CW00538118

The Brea

Peter Arnott was born in Gla
professional playwright with
Glasgow) and *White Rose* and *Elias Sawney* at the traverse (all
in 1985) he has written plays and songs (with Craig Armstrong),
cabaret (with Peter Mullan) as well as the occasional film and TV
script. He worked extensively with Wildcat Theatre Company,
writing, again with Peter Mullan, the Poll Tax musical *Harmony
Row* among others. His work has often had an historical focus,
including *Muir* and *The Wire Garden* along with comedies like
Losing Alec and his versions of modern European classics like
Durrenmatt's *The Visit* and Brecht's *Puntila*. More recently, his
trilogy of classic adaptations for the Citizens' Theatre's multi-
national community company have had great acclaim. His play
The Breathing House won the TMA Award for best new British
play of 2003. His most recent play *Cyprus* was specially
commissioned for Mull Theatre Company and transferred to the
Traflagar Studios in London in December 2005 and tours in
Scotland in 2007. His plays have also appeared in Cork, New
York, Melbourne and Moscow.

fairplay press

The Breathing House

by Peter Arnott

fairplay press

First published by fairplay press, an imprint of Capercaillie Books Limited in 2007.

Registered office 1 Rutland Court, Edinburgh.

© Peter Arnott. The moral right of the author has been asserted.

Printed in the UK.

A catalogue record for this book is available from the British Library.

ISBN 978-0-9551246-4-8

This book is sold subject to the condition that it shall not by way of trade or otherwise, be lent, resold, hired out or otherwise circulated without the publisher's prior consent in any form of binding or cover other than that in which it is published and without a similar condition including this condition being imposed on the subsequent purchaser. All rights reserved. No part of this publication may be reproduced, stored in a retrieval system or transmitted in any form or by any means, electronic, mechanical or otherwise without the written permission of the publisher. All applications for a licence to perform this play must be made before rehearsal to Capercaillie Books Limited. No performance may take place unless a licence has been obtained.

The publisher acknowledges support from the Scottish Arts Council towards the publication of this title.

Scottish **Arts** Council

Introduction

The Breathing House, produced at the Lyceum Theatre in Edinburgh in 2003, was a show where a lot of good things came together. Kenny Ireland found in the story what he wanted for his swan song as Artistic Director of the Lyceum. A big, elaborate, technically demanding entertainment that was all about Edinburgh, and needed twelve of the very best actors he could find, was how he wanted to take a bow. Consequently, it is one of the few experiences I've had in Scottish Theatre that was resourced to a level which truly demanded excellence.

From my point of view, it was a story I'd been waiting to tell for a very long time. Jeanette Foggo, appearing in a play of mine at the Tron in 1986, had given me a wonderfully illustrated book by Michael Hiley about Arthur Munby, a pioneer of photography in Victorian London, who had secretly married Hannah Culliwick, his servant and favourite model. Munby, in his innocent pre-Freudian way, had been obsessed with physically robust working women, at a time when women of his own class had affected tight lacing and vapours.

Inspired, I had tinkered with this story (and a contrasting story of a sexual relationship across classes, one rather more straightforwardly predatory in its inception, then complicated by the principals falling in love) for years, envisaging it for television and radio without success. I was very clear then that it was an Edinburgh story, or rather, a story set in Robert Louis Stevenson's Edinburgh of the Mind. A place of social experiment, ruthless and geographically expressed class warfare, all on an ancient rock from which breathed heaven knows what dark presences and darker memories. But it was just an idea till my ambitions coincided with Kenny's. That's the way it goes.

The National Theatre in London, at that particular moment, was keen to offer the use of its studio to provincial companies, so in the summer of 2002, we set off down south with a small company of actors, and the skeleton of a complicated Victorian 'Novel of Sensation', (as the rather disreputable end of the art form was known in those days) to improvise and play some games. Actors who would be in the show the next year were involved in this process. Forbes Masson, Kath Howden, Cora Bisset and Jeanette Foggo (who clung to this story as tenaciously as I did). We were also blessed by the presence of the remarkable Benny Young. Between us, with Kenny and me joining in, we put the human flesh on the conceptual bone, recording all of it on video. Some of what we filmed was great, and some of it can be used for blackmail purposes. But it all fed into the show, especially one movement based piece improvised by Matthew Scott on piano, and Benny Young and Kath Howden polishing a table, which was lifted straight into the finished play.

Kenny wanted to use Matthew, his long time collaborator (and devotee of Victorian popular music) to write an original score. That was very exciting. So was the inspired idea of asking Calum Colvin, one of Scotland's leading visual artists, whose work is based on the manipulation of staged images through the medium of photography, to design a flexible, beautiful set with two revolves and stunning, simple projections. Images from the show can be seen on Calum's website. He won an award for it, which was richly deserved, and hasn't been asked to design a show since, a neglect which he doesn't deserve at all.

These two made the play's world very real and very strange between them, achieving a tension between psychological abstraction and historical detail that exactly supported the text; and the theatre itself as a mid-Victorian edifice, became an extra, ambiguously gorgeous character in the show.

The play won the TMA Award for Best New Play of 2003. I've got the bit of glass in my house, but it was, like theatre always is when it really works, a collaboration. My thanks to all of the above.

Peter Arnott 2007

2

Characters

DR HENRY LITTLEJOHN: a social reformer.

ELIZABETH CHANTERELLE: his daughter and married to Gilbert Chanterelle.

GILBERT CHANTERELLE: her husband and medical researcher employed by Littlejohn.

JOHN CLOON: his friend, also a medical researcher and amateur photographer.

HANNAH WHITE: servant to John Cloon.

AGNES MCCUTCHEON: servant to Chanterelles.

RACHEL WHITE: Hannah's sister.

SORROW: Hannah's illegitimate daughter.

DAVEY: person of low morals who runs *The Breathing House* where Rachel and Sorrow reside.

The good people of Edinburgh themselves, Ministers, Whores, Trotter Scrapers and Pornogaphers, among others variously represented by members of the company.

Production Notes

First performed at The Royal Lyceum in 2003. Original Cast:

Cloon	Neil McKinven
Hannah	Kathryn Howden
Gilbert	Forbes Masson
Agnes	Cora Bisset
Littlejohn	Michael Mackenzie
Elizabeth/Annie	Jennifer Black
Rachel	Jeanette Foggo
Sorrow	Kirsty Mackay
Davey/Hawker	Ronnie Simon
Katie/Women	Jodie Campbell
Abercrombie/Minister/Doctor	Barrie Hunter
Juggler/Minister/Turnkey	Mark McDonnel
Directed by	Kenny Ireland
Designed by	Calum Colvin
Score by	Matthew Scott
Lighting by	Jeanine Davies

The play has a great many scene changes that are often fluid, one scene merging into the next, carrying the last thought of the preceding scene with it. In the original production this was achieved with light and recorded sound as well as two revolving stage areas and projections. Any potential producer will need to address this element of how the story is told. Whatever technical strategy is possible, a degree of abstraction in the settings is probably necessary. Whatever technical strategy is adopted or whatever the chosen style of production, a degree of abstraction in the settings is probably necessary.

Act 1

Scene 1

Edinburgh around 1860s. Cloon's house. HANNAH takes bloody sheets from a bed. Caroline Cloon is dead in a coffin standing on its end. JOHN CLOON is setting up a camera to photograph her. Looking on are his friends, GILBERT, ELIZABETH, and DR. LITTLEJOHN. LITTLEJOHN prompts GILBERT.

LITTLEJOHN: Distract him, will you?

GILBERT: Yes, sir. **(Pause. To CLOON.)** Life goes on, old fellow.

CLOON: Excuse me, Gilbert, I don't want to miss the light.

GILBERT: She looks very nice.

CLOON: Doesn't she?

He turns back to his work. GILBERT returns to ELIZABETH and LITTLEJOHN.

ELIZABETH: They should never have married.

GILBERT: Elizabeth, please . . .

ELIZABETH: She was never sufficiently robust. Whatever does he think he's doing?

GILBERT: Perhaps they were in love.

LITTLEJOHN: It's the hips, I'm afraid.

GILBERT: I beg your pardon.

LITTLEJOHN: The pelvic canal of the human female retains a gauge appropriate to a quadruped. With a smaller brain.

7

GILBERT: Does it?

ELIZABETH: Pretty little mouse.

LITTLEJOHN: Death in childbirth is the price that women pay for walking upright. Facts are facts.

GILBERT: I'm sure that thought will console our friend.

LITTLEJOHN: One cannot negotiate with evolution.

GILBERT: Particularly since he lost his child as well.

ELIZABETH: You needn't be offensive, Gilbert.

LITTLEJOHN: I'm not offended. And you're quite right, my dear. She was a nice little thing.

ELIZABETH: Dear Papa. **(To GILBERT.)** We should go to the Church now. **(She crosses to CLOON.)** We'll go now, John.

CLOON: Yes, thank you, Elizabeth. Doctor Littlejohn.

GILBERT: John, is there nothing we can do?

CLOON: **(puzzled)** Well, no, Gilbert. She's dead. **(Pause.)** I photographed our child, you see, in her little coffin. Caroline never liked me to take her photograph. But I feel I should like to have some record.

GILBERT: Shall I drive with you to the church?

CLOON: No, I'll see you there. Thank you.

ELIZABETH: Gilbert . . . shall we?

GILBERT: I'm so very sorry, John.

His visitors leave. CLOON walks to the coffin. HANNAH approaches.

HANNAH: I'm finished upstairs, sir. Will there be anything else?

CLOON: **(nods)** Help me, Hannah, please.

HANNAH helps him arrange Caroline for the photograph. He takes off his ring, and HANNAH takes it from him and places it on Caroline's finger. As he does he is arrested by the contrast between Caroline's hands and HANNAH's.

CLOON: Your have strong hands.

HANNAH: Thank you, sir.

CLOON goes under the cloth behind the camera. Music. As he removes the lens cover, he silently counts a ten second exposure and Caroline's image appears, inverted on a screen. CLOON replaces the lens cover. The image vanishes. Music ends. Pause. There is a bell ringing.

CLOON: Would you let them in, Hannah. Help them.

He takes the plate from the camera and exits. HANNAH looks at her hands. The bell rings again. HANNAH exits.

Scene 2

The Chanterelles' kitchen. The bell rings again. AGNES, the Chanterelle's maid, is on her knees, in tears at the kitchen table. The bell rings. She doesn't hear it. It rings again. AGNES continues to weep. After a moment, ELIZABETH, still dressed in mourning, comes in.

ELIZABETH: Agnes, didn't you hear me?

AGNES: **(standing)** I'm sorry, Ma'am. I didn't know ye were home yet.

ELIZABETH: Agnes . . . what's the matter?

AGNES: Nothing, Ma'am. Shall I help you get changed now?

ELIZABETH: Are you ill?

AGNES: No, Ma'am.

ELIZABETH: Has someone been upsetting you?

AGNES: No, Ma'am, I'm just being silly.

ELIZABETH: Have I upset you?

AGNES: Oh, no.

ELIZABETH: I try to be kind.

AGNES: You are kind.

ELIZABETH: Is your family well?

AGNES: Yes, Ma'am, so far as I know.

ELIZABETH: Agnes . . . sit down, here. **(AGNES sits. ELIZABETH kneels by her.)** Now, you're going to have to enlighten me sooner or later.

AGNES: I don't know what ye mean, Ma'am.

ELIZABETH: When I was twenty one, Agnes, there was only one thing in the world that could make me cry. **(She waits for an answer.)** You're not expecting, are you, Agnes?

AGNES: **(stunned, recovers)** No, Ma'am.

ELIZABETH: You would know, would you, you'd understand the signs?

AGNES: Yes, Ma'am. I'm not.

ELIZABETH: But you have been keeping company with a man, haven't you?

AGNES: Yes, Ma'am. **(The admission winds her.)**

ELIZABETH: You understand that if you were to fall pregnant,

Agnes, we couldn't keep you here? Even if you were to find a husband, we couldn't employ a married couple with a child.

AGNES: I'm not pregnant. I promise.

ELIZABETH: There's a good girl. So there's no harm done. You won't be seeing him again. **(AGNES hesitates.)** What is it?

AGNES: I've done wrong in your house.

ELIZABETH: **(sighs, pause)** You don't need to go into the details, Agnes. I'm really not interested in hearing your confession.

AGNES: I can't stop thinking about him.

ELIZABETH: Yes, you can.

AGNES: I can't.

ELIZABETH: You must.

AGNES: I can't.

ELIZABETH: You simply mustn't see him again.

AGNES: I can't help seeing him, Ma'am. I see him every day.

ELIZABETH: Agnes, you mustn't be obtuse. I know that you see my husband every day.

She waits.

AGNES: **(eventually)** Ma'am?

ELIZABETH: What you are not to do is to continue allowing my husband to have his way with you. Agnes, I don't want to lose my temper with you.

AGNES: No, Ma'am. **(She stares at ELIZABETH.)**

ELIZABETH: What is it?

AGNES: How did you know?

ELIZABETH: It's not a very large house. These things happen,

Agnes. On this occasion, without any uncomfortable issue. You're not to concern yourself any further. I shall speak to Mister Chanterelle. Go and wash your face.

AGNES: Are ye not upset?

ELIZABETH: Well, I should prefer it, naturally, if my husband didn't interfere with the servants. Now, I think we've said enough on the subject.

AGNES: Are ye not upset wi me?

ELIZABETH: I shall be extremely upset with you if you continue to ask me impertinent questions. What's wrong with you, girl? You don't imagine you're in love with him, do you? **(She waits. Then, astonished.)** Do you?

AGNES: I love him utterly.

ELIZABETH stares at her uncomprehendingly. The voices of LITTLEJOHN and GILBERT are heard offstage as they enter the house.

ELIZABETH: That's the gentlemen coming in from the cemetery. For goodness sake, compose yourself and serve tea in the small parlour.

AGNES: Yes, Ma'am.

Scene 3

Chanterelle house. Small parlour. Some moments later. LITTLEJOHN, GILBERT and ELIZABETH are served tea and cakes by AGNES who, as a servant, hears but must not respond. ELIZABETH plays on her hidden distress.

ELIZABETH: **(taking tea from AGNES)** How was John, father? At the graveside.

LITTLEJOHN: Peculiar. It's that damned hobby of his. Photography! His late father thought as I do on that subject, I may tell you.

GILBERT: **(taking tea from AGNES)** It's the way of fathers to find the passions of their offspring peculiar.

ELIZABETH: Not only offspring.

GILBERT glances at her. He becomes aware of AGNES' distress.

LITTLEJOHN: Aye, well wait till your wee ones are a little older, Gilbert, and then we can sensibly pursue this conversation. Will you be coming to the Club?

GILBERT: I thought I'd go and sit with John.

LITTLEJOHN: Don't indulge him, Gilbert.

GILBERT: An empty house, sir. It's no good. It can break your heart.

ELIZABETH: That's true, father. There's nothing so bad as an empty house. You desert us . . . for your clubs. Goodness knows what you get up to.

LITTLEJOHN: My dear, it's all perfectly respectable.

GILBERT: Perhaps you should come along one night. Dressed as a boy.

ELIZABETH: Oh, no thank you, I'm not at all curious.

LITTLEJOHN: **(rising, to GILBERT)** . . . if you change your mind. **(He kisses ELIZABETH.)** Good night, my dear. **(Noticing.)** You're not changed yet.

ELIZABETH: Thank you for noticing, father. No. Agnes is not herself tonight.

LITTLEJOHN: She looks very bonny to me. **(He touches her cheek.)** Rude, good health. Strong bones, good skin . . . eh, Agnes?

AGNES: Thank you, sir.

ELIZABETH: I had to ring for her four times.

LITTLEJOHN: **(to AGNES)** I'd batten down the hatches if I were you.

AGNES: Yes, sir.

LITTLEJOHN: **(to GILBERT)** Take care of John. He may be peculiar but he's conscientious. You may study him in that particular.

GILBERT: Good night, sir.

Exit LITTLEJOHN.

AGNES: Will there be anything else. Ma'am.

ELIZABETH: Wait in the kitchen, please.

AGNES exits.

GILBERT: What's the matter with Agnes?

ELIZABETH: Do you find her biddable, Gilbert? **(Pause.)** I'm afraid I must ask you to make a decision with me.

GILBERT: About Agnes? Surely that's your . . .

ELIZABETH: Domain. Yes.

GILBERT: Do you want me to dismiss her? Do you want me to write a character for her?

ELIZABETH: I want you to dismiss her. But she is to have no character.

GILBERT: What will she do without a reference, poor thing?

ELIZABETH: Agnes is disturbed.

GILBERT: Disturbed?

ELIZABETH: I really think she might be dangerous. We can hardly recommend a dangerous servant to our friends.

GILBERT: Elizabeth? Dangerous? Agnes?

ELIZABETH: She's imagining things.

GILBERT: She doesn't look mad to me.

ELIZABETH: But it's you that she's mad about, Gilbert. She seems to imagine that she is having a love affair with you.

GILBERT: With me?

ELIZABETH: She has persuaded herself that she is in love with you. Utterly. That was her exact expression.

GILBERT: She told you this?

ELIZABETH: Yes.

GILBERT: Well, you're right, it is extraordinary of her.

ELIZABETH: She's quite clearly deluded.

GILBERT: Yes.

ELIZABETH: 'I love him utterly.'

GILBERT: Yes.

ELIZABETH: She is to have no character.

GILBERT: **(nods)** No, of course not. I'll speak to her.

He goes to exit.

ELIZABETH: Don't be cruel to her, Gilbert. It's really not her fault, is it?

GILBERT: No.

ELIZABETH: You must try not to be quite so fascinating in the future.

GILBERT: Yes.

GILBERT exits parlour and meets AGNES on another part of the stage as the scene changes to the street around them. They embrace. The scene change continues. AGNES weeps. ELIZABETH looks down.

Scene 4

CLOONS house. CLOON sits at a table set for two. HANNAH enters.

HANNAH: Should I serve you now, sir?

CLOON: Yes. Thank you, Hannah.

She exits returning with a soup tureen. She serves him. She goes to a sideboard and pours him a glass of wine.

CLOON: It's been a tremendous help having you with us these last few months, Hannah.

HANNAH: Thank you, sir.

CLOON: Caroline became very fond of you.

HANNAH: Thank you, sir.

CLOON: There's plenty of soup.

HANNAH: Yes, sir.

CLOON: I don't think we can expect Mister Chanterelle now.

HANNAH begins to clear the empty place.

CLOON: I wonder if you'd like to stay on. Employed here.

HANNAH: Yes, sir. Thank you, sir.

CLOON: Thank you, Hannah.

She exits, taking the tureen. CLOON eats his soup.

Scene 5

Street. AGNES and GILBERT hurry through darkening streets.

AGNES: Where are we going?

GILBERT: Why did you tell her?

AGNES: She already knew. Where are we going?

GILBERT: She didn't know until you told her.

AGNES: Yes, she did. She knew everything.

GILBERT: My wife is not a witch. My wife is not the wise woman of Sarawak.

AGNES: She's very clever.

GILBERT: She's certainly cleverer than I am.

AGNES: Do you not think you could find me another position?

GILBERT: Gentlemen do not arrange employment for ladies' maids. Edinburgh smells a rat where that kind of thing is concerned.

AGNES: I love you.

GILBERT: Stop saying that.

AGNES: But it's true.

GILBERT: You are holding a gun to my head. Do you understand that? You are holding a gun to my head.

They stop at a door. Darkness. Breathing.

AGNES: What's this place?

GILBERT: I can visit you here.

AGNES: A place for me? A room

GILBERT: I suppose so . . .

AGNES: Oh, Gilbert!

She hugs him.

GILBERT: Please, Agnes. It's not three furnished rooms in Stockbridge. I'm not a wealthy man.

AGNES: But my own place!

GILBERT: Agnes, please. . . . You might have to make do a little.

He knocks at the door, a code. A panel opens. It closes. The door opens. DAVEY appears with a lamp. Breathing continues.

DAVEY: Mister French.

GILBERT: I need a room. A private room.

DAVEY: All night? Or just for the hour?

AGNES: Mister Chanterelle . . .

GILBERT: No names, you are not to use my name here.

AGNES: What kind of place is this?

GILBERT: **(to DAVEY)** I can pay you a week in advance.

DAVEY: A week?

AGNES: No.

GILBERT: What should I do? Where else are ye going to go? Shall I send you back to your father? Shall we book into the North British Hotel?

AGNES: I'm not going to stay in a brothel!

DAVEY: This is a lodging house, Miss. Among other things. Discreet. Accommodating. There are several ladies of quality here, squirrelled away from the eyes of the world. There is a tannery on a lower floor. There are places of entertainment, and on Sundays, there is the singing of sweet Christian ladies. You'll be quite comfortable here. Quite safe. This way, please.

DAVEY leads them into the dark, through a labyrinth of corridors. Doors sometimes open, flooding the stage with light, each revealing a strange vignette. Then they go into darkness again. They come to another door.

DAVEY: One moment, please. **(Davey goes into a room. There is noise as he drags a woman, who is stoned, out of the darkness.)** On ye come, Bella . . .

BELLA leans on a pillar.

DAVEY: I can leave you a lamp.

GILBERT: **(to AGNES)** Don't be frightened. **(To DAVEY.)** Could you leave us for a moment?

DAVEY: You'd not find your way out, sir. Not from here.

GILBERT: Agnes, do ye trust me.

AGNES: I hate this place.

DAVEY: It's all very different in the daytime, Miss.

19

AGNES: Yer no gonnae leave me here.

GILBERT: I must. I will come and see you tomorrow. Agnes. This is hard for me too.

AGNES: Yes, sir.

GILBERT: **(to DAVEY)** A week then. And the lamp, please.

DAVEY: That's another fourpence for the lamp, sir.

GILBERT pays him. They close the door on AGNES. As they leave.

GILBERT: You're to keep her safe. You're to tell no one she is here.

DAVEY: Everything is secret, Mr French.

DAVEY leads GILBERT away. AGNES is left with her lamp. The sound of breathing.

Scene 6

CLOON'S house. HANNAH is scrubbing the floor. CLOON watches. She tries not to let his scrutiny bother her. He continues to watch. She looks up at him.

HANNAH: Can I help you, sir?

CLOON: Yes. I want to ask you something.

HANNAH: Ask me what you like, sir.

CLOON: Well, then. I would very much like it if I could have your picture.

HANNAH: My picture, sir?

CLOON: Yes . . . you know my hobby . . .

HANNAH: Yes, sir.

CLOON: I should like to capture . . . your image. I know that sounds intrusive.

HANNAH: No, sir.

CLOON: Are you sure?

HANNAH: It's no gonnae hurt me. I've had my picture taken before.

CLOON: But a photograph can be much *more* than a likeness, Hannah. I mean a good photograph. If the eyes meet the lens in just the right way . . . they can speak. I'm not expressing myself. We live in a world where we present ourselves . . . a photograph . . . can reach beyond appearance . . . somehow . . . it can tell the truth.

HANNAH: Shall I get changed, sir.

CLOON: No, Hannah . . . I should like to photograph you at your work.

HANNAH: I'm all dirty.

CLOON: Yes.

HANNAH: I'm a cowp.

CLOON: No, no. There is a nobility . . . in your dirt.

HANNAH: **(laughs)** Beg your pardon, sir. But that's a funny kind of thing to say to anybody.

CLOON: Wait till you see. Could you stay there a moment?

CLOON exits. HANNAH kneels, puzzled but not unexcited. CLOON returns with his camera and tripod. He starts to shorten the tripod legs.

HANNAH: Can I help you, sir?

CLOON: No. Thank you. You're my subject now, not my servant.

HANNAH: Would it not be easier if I stood up?

CLOON: You can't scrub the floor standing up. **(The camera is ready. CLOON turns his attention to HANNAH.)** Now, could you scrub please.

HANNAH: **(she giggles)** I'm sorry.

CLOON: No, your smile is charming.

That comment crossed a line. They both know it. They both retreat back over it.

CLOON: Now. **(HANNAH starts scrubbing.)** What is it you're using there?

HANNAH: It's a Lye Soap, sir.

CLOON: An Alkaline?

HANNAH: If you say so, sir.

CLOON: Doesn't it hurt your hands?

HANNAH: Aye, sir. It does. But it shifts the stour.

CLOON: Could you stop, I mean . . . assume an attitude . . . oh, dear . . .

HANNAH: You mean like this?

She poses for the camera, to some advantage.

CLOON: **(taken aback)** Yes. Exactly like that. **(He moves under the camera.)** That's perfect, now the light isn't too good, so I shall need a fifteen second exposure. Do you think you can stay like that.

HANNAH: Yes.

CLOON: Now.

Photograph music, as before. CLOON removes the lens cover. He quietly counts to fifteen as HANNAH poses. Her image is projected, upside down. CLOON replaces the cover. The image vanishes.

HANNAH: What happens now, Sir?

CLOON: Well . . . would you like to see?

HANNAH: Yes, Sir. I mean, if I may.

CLOON: Of course. I've seen you do your work, now you should
　　　see mine. **(He takes the plate in its cover from the back of
　　　the camera.)** Come.

He holds out his hand. She takes it and he helps her to her feet. He smiles awkwardly.

HANNAH: Thank you, sir.

Scene 7

Dark room. Darkness. CLOON and HANNAH come into the dark room. He has a lamp with a red shade. That is the only light.

CLOON: Of course, this isn't my work, properly speaking. But it
　　　is rather my passion.

HANNAH: Yes, sir. I know, I've noticed all the pictures in your
　　　study.

CLOON: Have you looked at them?

HANNAH: Yes, sir. You like to photograph women.

CLOON: Yes.

HANNAH: Women like me. Working.

CLOON: Yes.

HANNAH: It's all right. There's no reason you shouldn't. **(Pause.)** What do we do now?

CLOON: Well . . . what we do is this . . . it's not unlike doing the washing . . . I'm sorry, that's sounds silly . . .

HANNAH: Please, sir.

CLOON: Well, we first bathe the image in this tank . . . to fix it.

HANNAH: Why is there a red light.

CLOON: Oh, well you see, the glass is treated with a chemical that is sensitive to light, and your image would be bleached out . . . by any light but this.

HANNAH: Why does it have to be red?

CLOON: I don't know . . . it's something to do with wavelengths. Light is made of waves . . . I'm not a scientist . . . **(He puts the plate in a second bath.)** But this is where the magic happens. Look.

HANNAH: I don't see anything.

CLOON: Wait.

As they watch, HANNAH's image appears on the paper, and we see it as it does, projected. Reprise photograph music. Music ends.

HANNAH: That's . . .

CLOON: Yes. That's you. I think it's come out rather well. The shapes, the contrast of light and shade, no, I'm very pleased. Yes.

HANNAH: That's me.

CLOON: Do you like it?

HANNAH: I don't know.

CLOON: Caroline . . . didn't like me to take her picture.

HANNAH: Why. . . if I can ask.

CLOON: She didn't like the way she looked . . . she had a horror . . . of the physical . . . of bodily processes . . . which was why the way she died was so . . . appalling. She died . . . hating herself.

HANNAH: She was very . . . delicate. Pretty. **(She indicates the picture.)** Not like me.

CLOON: You look . . . honest.

HANNAH: D'ye think so?

CLOON: Yes. **(Noting her engagement with his thought.)** Do you like what you see?

HANNAH: I don't know.

CLOON: It will never change. That's one thing. I mean, that's you there, forever. Never aging. Never changing.

HANNAH: It's not really me, then

CLOON: But it is. The truth of you. At that moment . . .

HANNAH: But I'll be gone, won't I?

CLOON: I shall treasure this.

They look at each other. The pause stretches into awkwardness.

HANNAH: I'd better be getting back to that floor. Ye cannae leave that stuff on it owre long. It's ceramic.

He pegs the picture on a string to dry.

HANNAH: **(self-conscious)** It is a bit like doing the washing.

She exits.

Scene 8

Princes Street Gardens. HANNAH leads a girl aged about ten to a spot to have a picnic. HANNAH carries a basket. The girl holds a new doll. HANNAH lays down a blanket and opens the basket. The girl, called SORROW, looks in.

SORROW: What's all this?

HANNAH: Well I thought it would be nice for us to have a picnic today, seeing as we're going to be looking at all the ladies and gentlemen.

SORROW: But you've got me this dolly already.

HANNAH: I know. Have ye thought of a name for her yet?

SORROW: Milly.

HANNAH: That's a good name. Would ye like a wee sandwich?

SORROW: **(eating)** Wha's the name of this place, Auntie Hannah?

HANNAH: Don't talk with your mouth full. Try again.

SORROW: What's this place we're looking at.

HANNAH: Well, it's a big new shop for all the Ladies and Gentlemen to get their nice things in. But ye see, instead of going to all different shops for linen and china and boots and things, now they can go to one big shop.

HANNAH takes a bite of sandwich.

SORROW: What are they gonnae call it?

HANNAH: **(chewing)** *Jenners*.

SORROW: Can we go there?

HANNAH: Mebbe one day.

SORROW: Are you rich, Auntie Hannah?

HANNAH: No.

SORROW: But ye've got me all these things. I bet you could go in there and get whatever you want. Do they have toys in there?

HANNAH: I think they have everything in there. Look at the people. See how tall and proud they are.

SORROW: I'm tall. Hannah. Are ye as tall as me.

They stand and see.

SORROW: Nearly. So, can I come and stay wi you sometime soon?

HANNAH: Maybe one day.

SORROW: Can I not come and stay wi you and help wi yer work? I'm a good wee worker.

HANNAH: No, darlin'.

SORROW: Does Mister Cloon not like children.

HANNAH: Cloon. I don't know if he does or not.

SORROW: Is he nice?

HANNAH: He's very nice. We'll need tae get you back to . . . back to Rachel.

SORROW: Will ye ask Mister Cloon about me, see if I can come and stay. Tell him I'm a good worker.

HANNAH: Ye'll need to show me where to find this new place Rachel's in.

SORROW: I don't think I like it as much as the old place.

HANNAH: Now, you mind yer Rachel. She's good tae you. Come on.

They get up. They walk. The town gets darker, more dangerous around them. They come to a door.

HANNAH: Sorrow, what is this place?

SORROW: This is where Mummy Rachel stays now. Wi her friends. Ye can hear them. Listen.

We now hear women's voices singing. Ethereal, beautiful. *The Sweet Sisters*.

RACHEL: *Who are you, sisters, what made you? What are you made of? Are you mud? Are you the rib of a man? You are created souls, created souls. You are no monkey's daughter. Did you evolve, sisters, that's what they call it, did you evolve, were you made from mud in a volcanic pool, are you a frog, are you a rib, no, you are a soul, you are a created soul. Sisters you are loved, God created you, he made you, he loves you, he cares for you, no matter what your sin, no matter what your wrong, you are his, you are made, you are loved, you are beautiful. Consider the lilies of the field, how much sweeter are you that are more sweet than the least of these. You are sweet, my sisters, you are sweet!*

Scene 9

RACHEL's room. Rachel sits in her room. HANNAH enters with SORROW.

HANNAH: Here we are.

RACHEL: So ye are. Hannah . . . how are ye, yer looking tired.

HANNAH: I'm not tired, I'm very well. There's a lot of stairs.

RACHEL: Can I make anything for ye?

HANNAH: No. No. Here. **(She gives her money.)** I've a wee bit more coming in now. I've more responsibilities.

RACHEL: Ye still with Mister Cloon?

HANNAH: Yes. I'm to stay. For the moment.

RACHEL: Oh, yer a family servant now.

HANNAH: He doesn't have a family anymore. His wife died. Some months ago.

RACHEL: Yes. She did.

HANNAH: I'd like to get that dress, Rachel, the one I left wi you.

RACHEL: Yes. If you like. **(She goes to a trunk and gets the dress out.)** Here.

SORROW: Oh, I like you in that. You havenae had that on for ages.

HANNAH: Why have ye come to this place, Rachel?

RACHEL: It's where God wants us to be. There are many poor souls here. Many children to be looked after, unwanted. We look after them. So don't worry about Sorrow. She has lots of new friends. Don't you, Sorrow?

SORROW: Yes.

RACHEL: **(holds up the money HANNAH gave her)** And this will help us to do our work. Thank you.

HANNAH: Sorrow, will you leave us a wee minute, we've something to talk about.

SORROW: All right. **(She kisses HANNAH.)** Will I see ye again soon?

HANNAH: I've another day off next week.

SORROW smiles and exits.

RACHEL: What's the matter, Hannah?

HANNAH: That money's for my daughter. That's for you and my daughter. It's not for any 'work'.

RACHEL: What is good for Jesus . . .

HANNAH: No, Rachel.

RACHEL: Are you being tempted, Hannah?

HANNAH: Tempted by what? What do you mean?

RACHEL: Sorrow. Do you want her back?

HANNAH: Of course I do.

RACHEL: Have you forgotten your shame?

HANNAH: One day, Rachel, I will tell her the truth. When I can. When I'm ready. **(She stands.)** I'll need to be going. Don't make her pray too much.

RACHEL: I don't make her pray. She likes to pray.

HANNAH: Please, Rachel, you know I'm grateful to ye . . .

RACHEL: When God wants her, He will come to her. She prays for you, Hannah. I pray for you too.

RACHEL gives HANNAH the dress.

HANNAH: Thank you.

HANNAH exits. RACHEL calls after her.

RACHEL: Don't be angry, Hannah.

HANNAH: I'm not.

Scene 10

As they part, GILBERT passes them on the stair. HANNAH thinks she recognises him, but he gives no sign of knowing her.

GILBERT makes his way up stairs, HANNAH down. They both get glimpses of strange little theatres of the soul. People costumed. Using drugs. HANNAH exits. GILBERT meets a masked gentleman on the stairs. He is drunk.

MASKED GENTLEMAN: Mister French! Going upstairs to see Rapunzel, are we?

GILBERT: Excuse me?

MASKED GENTLEMAN: What are you hiding up there, the Lady of Shallot? Is she, Mister French? She must be very special.

GILBERT: Get away from me.

MASKED GENTLEMAN: You should share, Mister French. Don't tell me you're in love.

He proceeds up stairs to AGNES room.

Scene 11

AGNES' room. AGNES is drinking. GILBERT knocks on her door. She leaps to it.

AGNES: I've tellt ye tae fuck off, haven't I?

GILBERT: Agnes?

AGNES realises her mistake and hides the bottle before opening the door.

AGNES: Mister Chanterelle. Come in. I'm sorry . . .

GILBERT: Are you all right?

AGNES: Yes, I'm fine. . . there was somebody by last night . . . I thought he was knocking again. I mebbe just imagined it.

GILBERT: Close your eyes.

AGNES: Why?

GILBERT: I've got a present for you.

AGNES: **(closes her eyes)** What?

GILBERT gives her charcoals and drawing paper.

GILBERT: Open them.

She does and is delighted.

AGNES: Thank you.

GILBERT: I remembered that you like to draw.

AGNES: Thank you.

GILBERT: It's little enough. It's not as if you have a window.

AGNES: Let me draw you.

GILBERT: All right. I've brought some wine, and cheese and things.

AGNES: Try and stay still. **(She starts to draw him. He can't keep still.)** Is something wrong?

GILBERT: How are you settling in now?

AGNES: I'm not so bad as I was.

GILBERT: Is that as favourable as you can be about it?

AGNES: I don't want you to be cross wi me.

GILBERT: I'm not cross with you. I'm sorry. **(Pause.)** This is ghastly.

AGNES: It's no that bad, I mean I've got it to myself, there's families in this house fifteen to a room what wi the lodgers . . .

GILBERT: I didn't mean for you. **(He winces at himself.)** Well . . . I mean . . . **(Bridling at himself.)** Why can't I just say what I mean?

AGNES: **(trying to help)** It's no as nice as it was in your house, but I've kennt worse.

GILBERT: Yes. There's many people. . . would envy us.

AGNES: I think ye should smile. For yer picture. Ye'll make yerself feel better if ye smile. That's what I used tae do when I was scrubbing your kitchen floor, I used tae smile and make myself feel better. It works. **(She smiles.)** See.

GILBERT: Agnes, did you always want to talk?

AGNES: Oh, is it other things ye want to remember about me?

GILBERT: What other things?

AGNES: I remember. I used tae lie in my bed up in that attic, and just wait for the sound of you coming up the stairs. There was that one stair near the top that used tae creak. See when I heard that creak, oh, just the sound ae it used tae make me go aw soft just waiting for ye . . .

She comes over to him.

GILBERT: Stop it!

AGNES: I'm gettin aw excited, I cannae help myself.

GILBERT: Will you stop playing the whore!

AGNES: What?

GILBERT: The whore. The whore.

AGNES: I'm not a whore.

GILBERT: Then stop behaving like one. Do you think that's what I want?

AGNES: What do you want?

GILBERT: All this sex talk and standing there like that.

AGNES: Gilbert, I'm not doing anything.

GILBERT: Don't use my name.

AGNES: **(bewildered)** Why?

GILBERT: Why do you do that? Why do you pretend to be a whore? Are you trying to excite me?

AGNES: I'm excited.

GILBERT: You don't excite me any more.

She starts to cry.

GILBERT: Tears now. I can get tears at home, thank you. I can cry too. Watch me. **(False tears.)** Oh, I'm sad, make me feel better.

AGNES: You're acting.

GILBERT: Yes.

AGNES: I'm not acting. I don't know how to act.

GILBERT: Yes, you do.

AGNES: I don't.

GILBERT: Everyone's acting, Agnes. As if there was somebody watching. **(He points at her.)** You. You swung your hips when you served the tea. We all have mirrors in our head, don't you know that?

AGNES: Mirrors in our heads?

GILBERT: Don't lie to me. Don't play the simple little country girl with me. I've had you in my bed and I know better.

AGNES: I've never lied to you.

GILBERT: You've never lied to me?

AGNES: No.

GILBERT: I've lied to you.

AGNES: When?

GILBERT: When I told you I loved you.

AGNES: You've never said that. You've never told me that.

GILBERT: I must have done, surely.

AGNES: No.

GILBERT: You've said it so often to me.

AGNES: It's true . . . I do love you.

GILBERT: Then I love you. I love you. I love you. There. Three times. It's easy. It's easy to lie.

AGNES: Yes

GILBERT: Do you know the difference between the truth and a lie?

AGNES: Yes.

GILBERT: Do you?

AGNES: Yes.

GILBERT: So you can tell when I'm lying to you?

AGNES: Yes. You do love me. You do. You cannae help it.

GILBERT: **(pause)** You really are mad, aren't you?

AGNES: Yes.

GILBERT: I can't support you anymore.

AGNES: No.

GILBERT: You think I'm rich. I'm not rich.

AGNES: No.

GILBERT: They laugh at me in here? Did you know that?

AGNES: Do they?

GILBERT: They wonder what kind of princess you must be. Locked up in the tower, untouched by human hand.

AGNES: Yes. I'm grateful.

GILBERT: I should just forget about you.

AGNES: Yes.

GILBERT: Next time somebody knocks at your door, Agnes . . . let them in.

AGNES: Yes.

GILBERT: Don't keep saying that. I'm hurting you.

AGNES: Yes.

GILBERT: Do you want me to hurt you?

AGNES: No.

GILBERT: **(throws her money)** Then I won't. That's your rent till the end of the week. Find yourself another place. Do you understand?

AGNES: Yes, sir. I understand.

GILBERT: Is that all you have to say?

AGNES: Yes.

GILBERT retires from the field. AGNES watches him go.

Scene 12

CLOON'S house, the kitchen. Music. Time is passing. HANNAH is at her household tasks. At the moment she is scouring and then polishing a table. As she works, sometimes CLOON comes in to the room and watches her for a moment. Then he leaves. She tries not to register that she knows he is coming and going. He comes in a second time, paying close attention to her physical strength. She mops sweat with a cloth and it drops on the floor. He picks it up and gives it to her. Their eyes meet. He leaves the room. She continues working, polishing now. He returns. He can smell the polish. He sniffs. She turns. He smiles. She smiles back. He leaves. She mutters reprovingly to herself. She is now sweeping the table with a chamois, big movements, stretching her over the table. He returns. He stands close behind her. She becomes hesitant in her movements. Her hand holding the chamois stops. He puts his hand on hers. And then they are polishing the table together. Big, sweeping movements. He turns her round and she is in his arms, hesitant, but drawn to him. They struggle with themselves. Then they stand still, holding each other.

Scene 13

Meeting Hall. LITTLEJOHN addresses a public meeting, flanked by GILBERT, CLOON and ELIZABETH.

LITTLEJOHN: Ladies and Gentlemen. For years now, the good people of Edinburgh have suffered from anecdotes. We have bemoaned the division of our city, told each other tales of squalor and surprise, stepped up to avoid the sewage seeping from the broken soil pipes beneath our streets, lamented the disgusting habits of our citizens, looked up instinctively, not to see the sky, but to evade a basin full of slops hurled from a window without so much as a *gardy loo*. For years we have coughed politely, handkerchiefs over our mouths at the sight of beggars in the streets, immorality and disease boiling within the medieval precincts of the Old Town, watched our servants and errant sons for what contagion they may inadvertently transmit across the North Bridge . . . and we have consoled ourselves that such misery is too diverse to quantify, too complex to amend, too uncertain to be saved. **(He slaps the figures.)** No longer. My first act as medical commissioner for the city, the first such appointment in these islands, was to commission an exact anatomy of our social despair. Ladies and Gentlemen, we are no longer able to take refuge in amazement at the ways of the world. The ways of the world have been numbered, catalogued and made known. **(He indicates CLOON and GILBERT.)** My colleagues, Mister Cloon and Mister Chanterelle have explored and discovered, compiled and annotated our shame. In six months we shall report our findings, and make our recommendations. And then, Ladies and Gentlemen, if we then choose not to act, not to make war on poverty, overcrowding, and a sanitation system unreformed since the Black Douglas hoisted his men up Castle Rock and Robert the Bruce made small talk with a spider, we will be unable to blame our inaction on our uncertainty. If we refuse to act when we have the facts before us, Ladies and Gentlemen, that refusal will be, henceforward, deliberate cruelty. If ignorance is willed, my fellow citizens, ignorance is crime. Thank you.

Scene 14

Street in Edinburgh. CLOON and GILBERT walking. CLOON recites figures.

CLOON: Cowgate East to South Bridge. Population last year, 1701, infants, 263. Death of infants under five years, 66. Sixty six.

GILBERT: I don't recognize any of this, you know.

CLOON: It's accurate, you can vouch for that yourself.

GILBERT: It's accurate . . . but it's not true. It's insufficient. It doesn't explain.

CLOON: Explain what?

GILBERT: Us. Tell me, John, do you really believe that the human race would be without sin if we had proper drainage facilities.

CLOON: I think it might help.

GILBERT: No amount of sanitation will remove the blackness from our souls.

CLOON: I didn't know that was the purpose of the survey.

GILBERT: I don't believe it. I don't believe that human beings are born good and simple and are made bad and complicated by insufficient water closets. I think this whole project is an exercise in futility. I don't think it will make us one jot happier.

CLOON: People will live longer. And better.

GILBERT: Why would more of us living longer make the world a better place?

CLOON: What a peculiar thing to say.

GILBERT: This is the most peculiar city, and there's nothing in these tables can begin to express how strange it is.

CLOON: Well, I wouldn't know . . . I've always lived here.

GILBERT: My father came here from Toulouse . . . which is a city where people make things. Like Glasgow, where people make things . . . but here?

CLOON: This is the capital . . . like Paris . . .

GILBERT: But in Paris there are Kings and Emperors for all these people to serve dinner to . . . what do we have here?

CLOON: Lawyers, I suppose . . .

GILBERT: You have a capital city without a country. You have a court with no King.

CLOON: But Edinburgh is here.

GILBERT: Yes it is. And the fear and pleasure it inspires are peculiarly intense . . .

CLOON: Do you think so?

GILBERT: Edinburgh is the most erotic city in the world.

CLOON: Edinburgh, Gilbert? Erotic?

GILBERT: Yes. Allow a stranger to educate you in the ways of your flesh.

CLOON: Good God, do you have to?

GILBERT: It's cold here. You bodies are wrapped . . . and you rage against your covering. Don't you?

CLOON: Do we?

GILBERT: From your covered flesh you radiate forbidden desires. Searching out pulses, touch, skin. . . . Sometimes I swear I could run amok in Charlotte Square, I could cast my trousers to the wind that blows off Calton Hill . . .

CLOON: You'd be arrested, Gilbert.

GILBERT: I have dreams of Edinburgh naked . . . I imagine lawyers and merchants walking on George Street in the buff, nodding politely, greeting each other, naked . . . perhaps wearing little moccasins to stop the pavement from chafeing their feet.

CLOON: I think you're forgetting the weather.

GILBERT: I see ladies' maids, dugs out, pushing prams, lowering their eyes, smiling politely. Withered matrons sidelong glancing at the endowments of the gentlemen who swagger proudly with their sticks, noting with approval the shades and tints of muffs that pass them in the street. 'Good Morning, Miss McQuorquondale. . . . Good Day to you, Doctor Farquar' . . .

CLOON: Gilbert . . .

GILBERT: All nude, waiting to throw each other in the bushes in Queen Street gardens, all of them together, all caution abandoned, little piles of moccasins by the shrubbery, the sounds of their rapture drowning out those bloody church bells with moans of ecstasy till at last, a great, universal explosion of relief . . . and all is still. Till once more they prowl on George Street, quite serene, with every eye peeled for the nearest tumble.

CLOON: Is that what you're thinking in the office? When you're looking out of the window?

GILBERT: Isn't everyone? All these gentlemen with their whores tucked away on Rose Street; don't they long for a bit of honest, public intercourse? I've told you. You are always confining yourself, to your study, to your work, behind the glass of that camera of yours. You should be living in the world.

CLOON: I thought I did.

GILBERT: When you married Caroline, I said to myself, he wants a companion for his cell.

CLOON: Gilbert, please don't speak ill of her.

GILBERT: You chose the quietest, most retiring . . .

CLOON: . . . never mind what I wanted.

GILBERT: You wanted peace. Silence. Look around you.

CLOON: At what?

GILBERT: What you're missing. I'm sure its very interesting and provocative that the population density of the Tron is three hundred and what was it.

CLOON: 352.6 per acre. With 109 street cesspools. For a total population of 11,636.

GILBERT: Well quite. People still laugh, you know. People still fall in love.

Pause.

CLOON: Gilbert?

GILBERT: What?

CLOON: I'd like you and Elizabeth and Doctor Littlejohn to come to dinner on Thursday.

GILBERT: Delightful. Why?

CLOON: I want to entertain again. It's been . . . half a year . . .

GILBERT: John. Your quiet little house. With your books. And your photographs, and Hannah, bustling away.

CLOON: Yes, I must get back. Are you going my way.

GILBERT: I'll see you in the morning.

Scene 15

Bar. Music. Some time later. GILBERT is drinking with cronies. Women are working on the men, getting them to buy drinks. AGNES is in a corner of the room, drunk, ostentatiously not looking at GILBERT. Music begins, a dance. One of the women wants Mister French (GILBERT) to dance with her. He doesn't dance. Another man dances with the woman. AGNES tries to cut in. She takes drink from a bottle in the man's hand. She looks at GILBERT, and drinks more, pretending not to care. The men and whores, predatory instincts awakened, feed her more drink, more than she wants. GILBERT looks away. She makes no appeal to him. She is encouraged to dance, wild, drunk, abandoned till she collapses. The man pours drink over her as she lies unconscious. GILBERT looks on, trying not to care. They leave her. Music ends. Silence.

Scene 16

RACHEL's room. A young girl, CORA holds a baby. DAVEY stands with his arm around her. RACHEL and SORROW stand in attitudes of prayerful piety.

DAVEY: **(to the girl)** This is the Lady I told ye about. Cora, this is the lady.

CORA: Hello.

RACHEL: Hello, Cora. Does your little baby have a name.

CORA: Name a Christ, look after him, will ye . . .

RACHEL: Do you have that little bit of money? **(CORA hesitates.)** Coming to me, your boy will come to Jesus. I've looked after many, many children. Look at Sorrow here. Is she not clean of skin and hardy of bone. Touch her, look at her bright eyes.

CORA: She wan of yours?

RACHEL: Her mother left her with me. **(CORA is in tears.)** No, you mustn't. It is no sin, no failure . . . you are being brave, hurting yourself so that your child may know peace and health. With all our other little ones.

CORA: I've got five pounds. It's in his blanket.

RACHEL: **(giving the baby to SORROW)** That's good, Cora. Jesus will thank you . . . and bless Sorrow's new little brother.

CORA: Can I visit him?

RACHEL: Well now, where would we be if we let everyone do that?

DAVEY: I'll see he's all right, Cora. But you need tae get back tae work.

CORA moves towards the child. DAVEY restrains her.

RACHEL: Best not.

DAVEY: Come on, Cora.

He leads her out.

SORROW: He's bonny.

RACHEL: What shall we call him? **(She strokes SORROW's hair. DAVEY re-enters.)** How is the poor child?

DAVEY: She'll be braw.

RACHEL: Sorrow . . . would you leave us a moment. Take the child to the others . . . show him to them . . . their little brother . . .

SORROW exits with the child.

DAVEY: **(aroused)** Tell me again.

RACHEL: We live in heaven. **(DAVEY takes her to him. As DAVEY makes love to her.)** While the body sins and suffers here on earth, our souls live in heaven. Our flesh is in a dark glass, mirrored, inverted. The body burns . . . the soul is calm, the body hurts, the soul sings, the body kills, the soul is born in glory. There's no need to worry . . . about hell and punishment. This is hell, this is darkness and shame . . . we purge ourselves on earth and our souls shine above, and illuminate the smiling face of Jesus. **(Pause. DAVEY looks in her face, spent.)** So there's no need to worry. D'ye see?

Scene 17

CLOON's house. Dinner party. CLOON is making a presentation of his photographs to LITTLEJOHN, ELIZABETH and GILBERT. The images are projected on a screen.

CLOON: **(commentating)** Here we see two pit brow girls in Newcraighall. You see the sieve? That is to sift for usable pieces of coal in the byng.

LITTLEJOHN: I didn't imagine they would be panning for gold with it, John.

The image changes.

CLOON: And here is a Miss Ann MacLaughlin holding a book and a letter . . . she wanted to hold something, I'm not sure why. This next one . . . **(The image changes.)** . . . is . . . well she wouldn't give her name, but she did insist on being taken with this improbable Arcadian background . . .

LITTLEJOHN: **(as he speaks the lights change and the image fades)** What exactly is the point of all this?

CLOON: I feel strongly that our work as census takers should be supplemented with images.

ELIZABETH: Of degradation?

CLOON: No, Elizabeth. Of hope. Of the people that our reforms of housing and sanitation may benefit, not because they are wretched . . . but because there is beauty in them.

ELIZABETH: Unlike you, John, to be so passionate. I approve. Father?

LITTLEJOHN: Very well, John. I'll make a small allowance for your expenses. But I must say I'm not sure that your idea of beauty would have persuaded Plato.

HANNAH brings lights.

CLOON: Thank you, sir.

LITTLEJOHN: I wouldn't mention it to the medical commissioners either if I were you.

CLOON: Shall we sit down?

They move to the dining table. HANNAH begins serving.

LITTLEJOHN: There is a school of thought, John, that we would better serve these people by deporting them rather than taking their photographs.

ELIZABETH: This country has already tipped its refuse into America and Australia. I understand they're full. Are you suggesting Madagascar?

LITTLEJOHN: Elizabeth . . .

ELIZABETH: Should we ask the King of Buganda to lease us a few acres where we may deposit our prostitutes and costermongers?

LITTLEJOHN: You might find that a great many of our paupers would be only too willing to go. There are coffin ships crammed to the gunnels every week at Leith docks. The numbers of the poor must be reduced . . . through emigration or otherwise . . .

ELIZABETH: Really, father, you are quite mad. You take an isolated piece of ill digested science and make of it a doctrine of extermination.

LITTLEJOHN: Natural selection . . .

ELIZABETH: Is natural, father . . .

LITTLEJOHN: There is a body of respectable, scientific opinion . . .

ELIZABETH: You and your friends cannot disguise your selfishness as 'scientific opinion' any more than your grandfathers could cloak their cupidity in God's Will.

LITTLEJOHN: I am merely reporting what is being talked about . . .

ELIZABETH: By comfortable men over pork bellies and cigars.

LITTLEJOHN: There are too many paupers.

ELIZABETH: Then make them better off, father.

LITTLEJOHN: **(to GILBERT)** Gilbert, will you tell your wife she is talking nonsense.

GILBERT: Not I, sir.

LITTLEJOHN: **(to CLOON)** The education of women, John, is a noble aspiration. Its consequences are intolerable. It makes husbands into weasels and sends fathers to their graves.

ELIZABETH: Blame yourself, father. You should have locked the door of the library.

LITTLEJOHN: **(to HANNAH)** What do you think, Hannah? Have you ever heard the like?

HANNAH: I think it must be a very fine thing to have so much to say, sir.

They laugh.

LITTLEJOHN: Well said, Hannah, Elizabeth does have an unconscionable amount to say for herself.

HANNAH: I didnae mean it like that, sir.

CLOON: I have been encouraging Hannah in her reading. **(Silenced, his guests stare at him.)** Yes. When there is time, in the evenings, when her other duties do not occupy her, we read together.

LITTLEJOHN: Really? And what do you read together?

CLOON: Well, we read the bible . . .

LITTLEJOHN: Of course.

GILBERT: Poor Hannah . . .

ELIZABETH: There are some very good stories . . .

CLOON: And the language, of course, is beautiful . . .

GILBERT: What else?

CLOON: Well . . .

GILBERT: What does Hannah like to read?

CLOON: Hannah enjoys . . .

GILBERT: Let her speak, John. Hannah? . . .

HANNAH: We've been reading . . . *Lady Audley's Secret.*

ELIZABETH: Mrs Braddon? John, is that suitable?

CLOON: It is rather exciting.

HANNAH: We take turn about. When we started, I used to only read a page, and Mister Cloon would finish the chapter when I got tired. But I'm more used to it now.

ELIZABETH: It's all murders and adultery and secret identities . . . **(She glances at LITTLEJOHN.)** I believe.

HANNAH: **(enthusiastic)** Yes, it's really good . . . but the ending isnae right, when they locked her up wi the nuns. I know she'd been wicked, but she didnae deserve that. She was just trying to look out for herself.

HANNAH look at her listeners, as if suddenly seeing their faces. CLOON is gazing adoringly, but she feels the complications in how the others are looking at her. She closes her eyes.

LITTLEJOHN: Well . . . it all sounds very lively. Thank you, Hannah

HANNAH: **(strangled)** Thank you, sir.

HANNAH exits.

ELIZABETH: I must say I'm surprised at you, John.

CLOON: Why?

GILBERT: **(knowingly)** I'm flabbergasted, old boy.

ELIZABETH: To read with a servant . . . and such stimulating material . . . It's inappropriate.

CLOON: I don't see why. She's a grown woman, she's very sensible.

ELIZABETH: But you're deceiving her.

CLOON: How so?

ELIZABETH: You are intimating affection.

CLOON: I do like her.

ELIZABETH: John, please.

GILBERT: What Elizabeth means . . . is that affection gives the illusion of equality. And equality gives the illusion of love.

CLOON: I think you underestimate her intelligence.

ELIZABETH: John . . .

CLOON: No, I think you do.

He rings a bell.

GILBERT: John, what are you doing?

HANNAH enters.

CLOON: HANNAH . . . you remember what we were discussing earlier.

HANNAH: I'm sorry, sir.

CLOON: Doctor Littlejohn was outlining some rather extreme ideas that are being put about for dealing with the problem of poverty. Now, some people are saying that the solution is that the poor should be discouraged from breeding, and that the most effective way to achieve this would be deportation. What do you think of that idea?

HANNAH: I'm sure I don't know anything about it.

CLOON: Do you think it practical? Or moral?

ELIZABETH: John . . .

HANNAH: I don't know anything about it, sir.

CLOON: But you do, you see. We talk about the poor, we survey them . . . but what do we really know? We see poor people, we count them, but we never ask them . . . what they think. Do you think it would be possible, do you think it would be desirable . . . such a scheme?

HANNAH pauses, stricken.

GILBERT: Never mind, Hannah . . .

CLOON: I do mind. Hannah, I know you to be a highly intelligent, sensitive woman, who has no trouble in talking . . . I would like to know what you think.

HANNAH: I'd need tae think about it. Will you excuse me please?

She exits.

LITTLEJOHN: **(rising, angry)** What on earth are you thinking of, John?

CLOON: She's a clever woman.

LITTLEJOHN: She's a clever servant. A good servant. And your clumsiness may have lost her. This is why you need a wife, John. To regulate your house. It's rather late . . .

CLOON: Yes, I'll . . .

LITTLEJOHN: We'll see ourselves out. I don't imagine poor Hannah is in any state.

CLOON: I'm sorry.

ELIZABETH: Good Night, John. Please tell Hannah that dinner was excellent. Good night.

She and LITTLEJOHN exit. GILBERT hisses to CLOON.

GILBERT: You sly dog . . .

CLOON: What do you mean?

GILBERT: Oh please! But, John, take the advice of bitter experience. It's no bloody good with servants . . . understand? Good God man, she isn't even pretty.

CLOON: What are you implying?

GILBERT: **(smiling)** Dear John. I never knew you had the makings of a liar. **(Laughs.)** Good Night.

He exits. CLOON sits awkwardly. HANNAH comes in, furious.

CLOON: Hannah, I'm sorry.

HANNAH: You made a fool of yourself. You didn't make a fool of me.

CLOON: I've said I'm sorry.

HANNAH: . . . didn't you see that woman looking at me?

CLOON: Mrs Chanterelle . . .

HANNAH: I feel like you'd thrown me in a machine.

CLOON: Now, Hannah . . . I thought you did well . . .

HANNAH: Oh, do you?

CLOON: I should not have asked you that question . . . your answer was quite proper. You said . . .

HANNAH: It's not what the monkey says that brings the customers, eh? It's the fact the monkey speaks at all. What do you think of me?

CLOON: You know how I admire you.

HANNAH: It was not proper.

CLOON: There is nothing improper about what happens between you and me.

HANNAH: Yes, there is.

CLOON: No, there can't be . . .

HANNAH: There is! I am shouting at you. You are my employer, you should be kicking my arse into the street.

CLOON: How you do express yourself!

HANNAH: Oh don't, don't you dare say I'm charming or I swear to God I will land this ashette on your well turned cheek. We can't go on.

CLOON: What are you saying?

HANNAH: I'll not be made a fool of for your friends. I'll not have them gossip about me in their airy, comfortable rooms.

CLOON: What do you mean?

HANNAH: They knew.

CLOON: They didn't know.

HANNAH: They knew. Your friend Mister Chanterelle, he knew.

CLOON: What do they know?

HANNAH: That when I put away my apron I fold it by your bed.

CLOON: They know nothing about it.

HANNAH: I'll not be humiliated.

CLOON: Are you ashamed of me? Hannah, I love you.

HANNAH: No, stop it, you're trying to confuse me.

CLOON: No, it's the clearest simplest thing under the sun. You have given me my life. In your eyes and in your arms I see myself reflected to my glory, and it is my only wish to make myself the man that you in your loving heart have taken me to be.

HANNAH: They know that you are sleeping with your servant.

CLOON: Perhaps they do.

HANNAH: It's commonplace enough.

CLOON: No. This is not common. This is a greater joy than any man deserves.

HANNAH: It's common. And I was a fool to think differently. I'm fond of you, Mister Cloon. You're a nice man, and a clever man . . . and a strange man, I'll not pretend I don't think that . . . but I'm your servant. It's all there is for me to be. You take my picture as a servant, you see me as a servant. That's who I am. Now, if you want me to stay here we must put an end to all that other foolishness.

CLOON: Could you? Could you end it?

HANNAH: Yes. All the reading lessons, and the talking and the . . . and the love.

CLOON: Could you?

HANNAH: Yes.

CLOON: Hannah. Be my wife.

HANNAH: Now don't be stupid.

CLOON: I've said it. I heard myself say it. I meant it. Be my wife. Please. I don't want to lose you. If you cannot love me and be my servant, then love me and be my wife.

HANNAH: You're cruel to say that to me. If you don't mean what you say. When you can throw me out in the street the moment you want to.

CLOON: I would lose my eyes, I would lose my limbs, before I would lose you. You're honest. You're strong and you're brave. You're uncommonly . . . kind. You make me strong . . . **(She turns away.)** I am a strange man, Hannah. I admit it. . . . I don't relish high society. . . . I love ideas, I love reading and pictures and music and I love you.

HANNAH: You don't know anything about me.

CLOON: I don't need to know any more than that. Will you have me, Hannah White. Will you be my wife?

HANNAH: I don't want to sit at your table. I don't want to mingle with your friends.

CLOON: We'll have our own table.

HANNAH: No one is to know. Just us.

CLOON: Please, Hannah? . . .

HANNAH: Secret. A deadly secret. You have to swear.

CLOON: I swear.

HANNAH: You know what that is, to swear . . . to give me your word?

CLOON: Yes.

HANNAH: Yes. Yes, I'll marry you. God help me.

CLOON: God will help you. He will.

HANNAH: He'd better. **(Recovering.)** I'll clear up the dinner things.

CLOON: Very well. I'll . . . I'll be upstairs . . .

HANNAH: I want my own room tonight. No . . . I don't . . . but I want to choose. I want to choose my own room if I want.

CLOON: Do you want that?

HANNAH: No.

CLOON: Thank you, Hannah. You've made me very happy.

HANNAH: Yes, Mr Cloon.

Act 2

Scene 1

ABERCROMBIE'S studio. ABERCROMBIE, a lame, leering man, owner of a photographic studio in the Grassmarket, ushers in Mister CLOON. Or tries to. CLOON is struggling to bring ANNIE, a trotter scraper, in to get her picture taken.

ABERCROMBIE: This way, Mister Cloon. **(He sees CLOON stuck in the doorway.)** Do you need a hand there, Mister Cloon?

CLOON: Not at all, thank you, Mister Abercrombie. **(To ANNIE.)** This way please, madame.

ANNIE: I doan like this ony merr. I'm gaun.

CLOON: Now, now . . .

ABERCROMBIE: **(to ANNIE)** There's nothing in here to be afraid of.

ANNIE: Who's that?

CLOON: That's Mister Abercrombie. He owns this establishment.

ANNIE: I doan wanni go in any establishment. **(HANNAH enters. To CLOON and HANNAH.)** You said youse were gonni take ma picture.

CLOON: Quite right, that's all . . .

ANNIE: I'm a good woman.

CLOON: I can see that.

HANNAH: Now, nane ae yer nonsense, Annie. We'll give ye twoppence.

ANNIE: I'm wantin fourpence noo.

CLOON: Sit down, madame, please.

ANNIE: **(sits, CLOON looks at her face)** What you lookin at?

CLOON: Your face.

ANNIE: I want fourpence.

ABERCROMBIE: Mister Cloon . . .

HANNAH: Mister Cloon wants to put you in the best light.

ANNIE: Is that the camera?

ABERCROMBIE: Mister Cloon . . .

ANNIE: **(to HANNAH)** I'm a good woman.

HANNAH: I know.

ABERCROMBIE: Mister Cloon . . .

CLOON: Yes, Mister Abercrombie . . .

ABERCROMBIE: If the gentleman is interested at all, I have an extensive collection of images . . .

CLOON: That's fine, Hannah . . .

HANNAH: **(to ANNIE)** Try and stay still.

ABERCROMBIE: Images of the female form . . .

CLOON: **(not listening)** I see.

ABERCROMBIE: . . . in all of its glory.

CLOON: That's fine, Mister Abercrombie.

ABERCROMBIE: When I say glory, I am speaking of the Greek variety . . . of drapery and so forth.

ANNIE: Here, I'm no daein any ae that.

ABERCROMBIE: **(to ANNIE)** I don't imagine you'd get fourpence for it anyway.

57

ANNIE: **(to HANNAH)** Here, what's he sayin that fer?

CLOON: Mister Abercrombie. I am proposing a photographic study of the varieties of female labourer here in the capital.

ABERCROMBIE: What for?

ANNIE: What fer?

CLOON: History, madame. You're about to be a monument.

ABERCROMBIE: Might I suggest, there's an ornamental young woman who has consented to model for me on several occasions. She might well be easier under the gentleman's scrutiny.

ANNIE: Under his whit?

CLOON: Yes, yes, Abercrombie, anything you say . . .

ABERCROMBIE exits.

CLOON: Now, Madame, would you kindly relax?

HANNAH: Look into the eye, Annie, at the front of the camera.

CLOON: Hannah . . . would you mind asking . . .

HANNAH: Annie . . .

CLOON: To relax.

HANNAH: Annie, look at me, look over at me. Tell me about yourself. What work are you doing today?

ANNIE: I'm scrapin trotters . . .

HANNAH: Who do you sell to, Annie?

ANNIE: Mister Quinn, the farrier . . .

HANNAH: He makes the scrapings intae fertilizer, does he?

ANNIE: Aye.

CLOON: That's fine, Hannah, now if she can be still . . .

HANNAH: Can ye stay still, Annie. Look at my engagement ring, here on my finger.

ANNIE: It's lovely.

HANNAH: Thank you, keep looking, don't talk.

CLOON counts out a ten second exposure. As he does, ANNIE's image appears on a screen.

CLOON: That's perfect, thank you, Hannah.

HANNAH: You should thank Annie.

CLOON: Yes. Of course, thank you so much.

HANNAH: Here's your fourpence. And we'll give you a copy.

CLOON: Hannah!

HANNAH: I think we should. Annie's never had her picture taken before. **(to ANNIE, leading her to the door.)** Come with me.

They exit. As they do, ABERCROMBIE enters from the other door with a cheerful young prostitute, slightly the worse for drink.

ABERCROMBIE: Here we are, Mister Cloon. This is Katie.

CLOON: Is Katie . . . a working woman?

KATIE: Am I a whit?

ABERCROMBIE: How do you mean, sir?

CLOON: Does she work with her hands?

Pause.

KATIE: Amang other things, Mister, aye.

KATIE peals with laughter. HANNAH re-enters.

CLOON: Mister Abercrombie, I'm afraid this young woman is not suitable for a study . . .

HANNAH: **(interrupting)** Why not?

CLOON: **(still to ABERCROMBIE)** . . . of labouring women in Edinburgh . . .

HANNAH: Why not?

CLOON: What do you mean why not?

HANNAH: She works, doesn't she? I bet she works very hard. **(To KATIE.)** Don't ye?

KATIE: Oh aye, missis. I'm on ma back aw day. What's yer rate, mister.

HANNAH: Fourpence.

CLOON: Hannah, we said tuppence . . .

KATIE: **(posing)** Dae I look like a tuppenny bit?

HANNAH: She has a nice face.

KATIE: Oh dae ah, Missis? You intae this caper anaw?

HANNAH: Yes.

KATIE: Does he want the two of us thegither, cos that's extra . . .

CLOON: I don't think you understand . . .

KATIE: How d'ye want me?

CLOON: Just against that pillar?

KATIE: **(a raunchy posture adopted)** Like this dae ye mean?

CLOON: Heavens, this won't do at all.

KATIE: Weel, I'm no leavin wioot ma fourpence, Mister . . .

CLOON: Very well, please be still.

KATIE: Which bit ae me d'ye want?

CLOON: Your face, madame.

KATIE: My face?

CLOON: Now kindly be still and look into the lens.

KATIE: **(fixing her hair)** Christ, I've met some funny buggers in ma time . . .

HANNAH: There, John. How's that?

CLOON: All right, sit down, let's get this over with.

Photograph music. KATIE sits and looks cheekily at the camera. But as she poses, and CLOON counts the exposure, a reflective mood seems to take her over. Her image appears, as before, on a screen.

CLOON: There.

Music ends.

KATIE: **(reacting against her trance)** Ye done, are ye. Ye gonnae take that hame the two of ye. Is it gonnae help the two of yez oot a bit? **(To HANNAH.)** Is this what gets him gaun?

HANNAH: **(giving her money)** Here. Would ye like us to send you a copy?

KATIE: And ruin my fuckin reputation? **(To CLOON, like he was daft.)** You are a wierdie, d'ye ken that? **(She indicates ABERCROMBIE.)** Give me a good straight pervert any day.

ABERCROMBIE: Katie, could you and I mebbe . . .

KATIE: **(contemptuously)** Fuck off!

She exits.

CLOON: That wasn't right.

HANNAH: She looked nice.

CLOON: My remit from the board of health specifically excludes prostitutes.

HANNAH: There's laundry women ae fifty will sell themselves for a ha'penny tae get a crib for the night. What do you think a prostitute is?

CLOON: I can hardly address their morality in a photograph. By working women I mean honest, strong women . . .

HANNAH: Like me? I'd dae it, John. I would. I'd sooner be a wee whore like her than end as a dead saint frozen in a doorway. Now do ye want me tae gang out and get ye anither yin . . . cos we're paid fer till six and it's no gone three.

CLOON: Very well, Hannah.

She exits.

ABERCROMBIE: You've a most unusual servant there, Mister Cloon.

CLOON: Yes . . .

ABERCROMBIE: Are ye interested in handcuffs at all?

CLOON: Good afternoon, Mister Abercrombie.

ABERCROMBIE exits. CLOON sighs and prepares the next plate.

Scene 2

CLOON's office. CLOON and GILBERT work at their desks.

GILBERT: Have you had the measles returns for Broughton yet . . . John?

CLOON: Gilbert. I want you to do me a great service.

GILBERT: Gladly. What?

CLOON: I want you as a witness. At my wedding.

GILBERT: What?

CLOON: I am to be married, Gilbert, to Hannah, on Tuesday week. I should like you to be my support.

GILBERT: Good God! Hannah? **(He laughs.)**

CLOON: Gilbert . . .

GILBERT: You're serious?

CLOON: Yes.

GILBERT: Why?

CLOON: I realise it's rather an unusual . . .

GILBERT: Is it to be in the Abbey?

CLOON: No . . . a Unitarian minister is to perform the ceremony in my house.

GILBERT: Really? . . . Hannah?

CLOON: She's the most wonderful woman in the world.

GILBERT: Why on earth should you want to marry her?

CLOON: To commit my soul to her.

GILBERT: My dear fellow, she'll have your silverware . . .

CLOON: Hannah is the most honest . . .

GILBERT: John . . .

CLOON: . . . open creature on God's Earth. She has no secrets from me, no designs upon me. She is exactly what she seems, in every particular.

GILBERT: Yes, yes, I'm sure she is.

CLOON: I love her, Gilbert. Utterly.

GILBERT: **(registers AGNES's word, then)** Why are you asking me?

CLOON: Why am I asking you what?

GILBERT: To be your witness.

CLOON: I am not seeking your advice, Gilbert . . .

GILBERT: Do you want my blessing . . .

CLOON: You're my friend.

GILBERT: Why not ask Elizabeth? Doctor Littlejohn. Your rich Uncle in Fife?

CLOON: You're my friend. And you already know . . . that Hannah and I . . .

GILBERT: Yes.

CLOON: And I believe you will be discreet.

GILBERT: Do you, now? I could ruin you with this.

CLOON: I trust you.

GILBERT: Why? Because you could ruin me?

CLOON: **(hesitates, then laughs)** Gilbert, I believe you're as mad as I am. I'm not thinking of ruin, I'm thinking of happiness.

GILBERT: **(pauses at an alien concept, then)** If it makes you happy.

CLOON: It does. You were saying?

GILBERT: Was I? What?

CLOON: **(hands him papers)** The measles return for Broughton, wasn't it?

GILBERT: God rot Broughton. What do I care about Broughton, or any other damn place?

CLOON: Shall we send out for cakes?

GILBERT: Cakes . . .

GILBERT returns to his work.

CLOON: You must think me a very dry stick.

GILBERT: Not at all. I can see that you're happy.

CLOON: Are you not content? With Elizabeth, your children?

GILBERT: Are you quite blind? Look at my face.

CLOON: Why should I look at your face?

GILBERT: What do you see?

CLOON: What am I looking for?

GILBERT: Fear.

CLOON: What have you got to be frightened of, Gilbert?

GILBERT: Memories . . .

CLOON: Memories of what?

GILBERT: **(laughs, then)** Do you really want to know?

CLOON: Perhaps not. I'm not a worldly man, Gilbert.

GILBERT: **(fighting his self pity, losing)** No. You're . . .

He takes CLOON's arm in his hand.

CLOON: What?

GILBERT: Substantial.

CLOON: **(alarmed)** Gilbert . . .

GILBERT: I can deny myself nothing, you see? If I want anything, I am compelled to take it.

CLOON: I don't understand.

GILBERT: In this world of lies, John, our desires are the only things we can truly believe in.

CLOON: I see.

GILBERT: No you don't.

CLOON: Perhaps . . . if you were more specific . . .

GILBERT: Oh, I can't be specific. You'd hate me, John. The truth would deny me your house, everybody's house. Only liars are welcome everywhere.

CLOON: Gilbert, you can't be so very wicked, surely.

GILBERT: **(smiles)** There are women who will do anything you want them to do. For money. For shelter, even. Who will pretend happy compliance . . . in anything . . . even in marriage, John.

CLOON: Gilbert. Are you trying to frighten me? About my marriage?

GILBERT: You don't know anything about anything. Do you?

CLOON: Perhaps you're right. Perhaps I don't care to know. Is that wrong?

GILBERT: **(stands)** Come with me. Get your coat.

CLOON: Where are we going?

GILBERT: You want my discretion? About your impending nuptials?

CLOON: Yes.

GILBERT: Then let me teach you what discretion means.

Scene 3

The Old Town. CLOON and GILBERT walk into darkening streets, a darkening world.

CLOON: Where are we going? You're being very mysterious.

GILBERT: We're going to my club.

CLOON: Yours is the New Club, isn't it?

GILBERT: Not *that* club, old fellow. This is a house with a door in College Wynd, though I suspect its corridors and labyrinths emerge in many places.

They stand before *The Breathing House*.

CLOON: What is this place? Why did you bring me here?

GILBERT: I came across it last year. Doctor Littlejohn had asked me to investigate an extraordinary incidence of birth and death all emanating, apparently, from the same address. He suspected fraud. **(He shakes his head.)** There is nowhere in Edinburgh, John, where so much life goes on, where so many children are born, where so many people die. Where so many come to ruin, to run mad, or commit a crime.

CLOON: That's fanciful, surely. A matter of mean population density . . . that's all . . .

He tails off. There is something about the place.

GILBERT: It seems to me, that for years I'd been hearing about this place . . . of a place somewhere . . . a house . . . whispers . . . I thought perhaps I'd found it.

CLOON: Found what?

GILBERT: Don't you know that any sin is permissible, provided only it is not spoken. Any crime is forgiven, if it remains silent. It is only to speak the truth that is unforgivable.

CLOON: Gilbert, we should go back to the office.

GILBERT: John, the house breathes. I swear it. You put your head to the wall, and listen. To all the souls in here. Can't you hear them. Feel the stone with your hand. **(He places CLOON's hand on the wall.)** It swells. It breathes. Aren't you curious about that?

He knocks at a door.

Scene 4

Opium Den. The door opens and the stage is washed with smoke and strange light. DAVEY appears, masked.

DAVEY: Welcome, travellers. What is it you seek?

GILBERT: We seek fire from the Dragon's Mouth.

DAVEY: I spy a stranger. **(To CLOON.)** Seek you the Dragon's kiss?

CLOON: Gilbert . . . what? . . .

GILBERT: Say 'I do' old fellow, it will save time.

CLOON: I do.

DAVEY: Sixpence, please.

CLOON: I . . .

GILBERT: Put your purse away, old man. 'The stranger is under my guidance.'

He pays.

DAVEY: The stranger is welcome.

A curtain is opened on a scene of debauchery. Men lying on divans, tended by whores.

CLOON: Gilbert, what is this place?

GILBERT: Shoosh. Take your ease.

CLOON: I don't want to take my ease in a place like this.

GILBERT: You can be someone else here. Or you can be nobody at all. I find that's the best.

CLOON: These men. I know these men.

GILBERT: No, you don't. And they don't know you. There is nobody here.

CLOON: Gilbert?

GILBERT: Draw upon the pipe, John. I promise you'll not regret it.

CLOON: These men? Here?

GILBERT: There is no 'here' here. Since the first spice boats sailed to Cathay, no word of this place has been spoken aloud. Here is blessed nowhere.

CLOON: No, thank you. You must excuse me.

DAVEY: Does the stranger wish to leave?

CLOON: Yes, I . . .

DAVEY: Tribute has been paid. The Dragon's breath awaits.

CLOON: I don't want to.

GILBERT: You must do as we do. That's our protection. Here is the lesson I promised you. To share in our discretion . . . our silence . . . you must share our sin.

CLOON: Are you threatening me, Gilbert?

GILBERT: I'm not here.

CLOON draws on the pipe. He coughs.

GILBERT: **(urgently)** My wedding present to you, John . . . a little truth . . . and don't tell me it doesn't thrill you, just a little.

GILBERT smokes and settles. CLOON staggers to his feet.

CLOON: I'm a beast.

GILBERT: There, there.

CLOON staggers into the street. GILBERT lies back.

Scene 5

RACHEL's room. Before the wedding. HANNAH, well dressed, is putting the finishing touches to SORROW, who is also nicely dressed. RACHEL is looking on.

SORROW: So will you and Mister Cloon be having children?

HANNAH: Perhaps.

SORROW: Will ye let me come and play wi them?

HANNAH: Yes. Of course.

RACHEL: Now, Sorrow, I don't think a gentleman like Mister Cloon would want a little girl like you inside his house.

HANNAH: He would.

RACHEL: Do you think so?

HANNAH: Yes. She's going to his house today, isn't she?

RACHEL: As a witness to your wedding . . . not to play. Not to live.

HANNAH: Sorrow. Will you give us a moment?

SORROW: Are you telling secrets, Auntie Hannah.

HANNAH: Try not to get dirty.

SORROW exits.

RACHEL: **(hisses)** Why are you putting this child in peril of her soul?

HANNAH: No one is in peril of anyone's soul.

RACHEL: You are going to marry a man, and you are denying your child.

HANNAH: I will tell him later. I will tell her. I'm to be the judge of this.

RACHEL: No, Hannah, it is not you who will be the Judge.

HANNAH: Then let *Him* judge me, and let you help me to get married.

RACHEL: Your marriage is a lie.

HANNAH: No. If I'm sure of anything, I'm sure of that.

RACHEL: You don't know if Sorrow's father is alive or dead.

HANNAH: I don't know who he was. There were four of them and it was dark. They nearly killed me. I let you look after Sorrow, I let you name her, not because I was ashamed of myself, but because I needed to work . . . and nobody hires servants with bastards . . .

RACHEL: Hannah . . .

HANNAH: We have to pretend, Rachel, if we are to go into the houses of ladies and gentlemen, we have to pretend that the world is what they think it is, we can't afford to upset them . . .

RACHEL: It's not an employer you are deceiving, it's a husband.

HANNAH: John is a good man. I have faith in him; that in time he will be wise, and he will understand. And he'll forgive me.

RACHEL: You're very cool. You're very precise on your bridal morning.

HANNAH: I do believe I'm honest. Help, me Rachel. Be my sister. You don't have to approve of me to see that this is what I want.

RACHEL: **(considers, then)** Sorrow should be there. I will accompany her.

HANNAH: **(hurt, accepting)** Yes. Well, thank you. Shall we go?

HANNAH exits. RACHEL hesitates. She prays angrily and quietly for a moment. Then follows.

Scene 6

CLOON's house: the wedding. The MINISTER stands between CLOON and HANNAH.

MINISTER: Before the sight of God, and by the power given me, I now pronounce you man and wife.

GILBERT: Congratulations, old fellow. Hannah.

SORROW: Congratulations, Auntie Hannah.

GILBERT: Thank you, Minister, a lovely . . . **(With a glance at CLOON.)** . . . discreet little ceremony.

CLOON: **(to the MINISTER)** Please, won't you stay for a drink?

MINISTER: Mister Cloon, I really should be going.

CLOON: Are you sure?

MINISTER: I fear so, I am pressed for time.

CLOON: Let me see you out. Hannah, would you serve drinks, my dear?

HANNAH: Yes, John.

CLOON exits with the MINISTER. HANNAH exits to get the drink. GILBERT and HANNAH's family look at each other.

RACHEL: Haven't I seen you somewhere before?

GILBERT: This is your daughter, is it?

RACHEL: This is Sorrow.

GILBERT: It's a very unusual name.

RACHEL: Your name is French, isn't it?

GILBERT stares at her a moment. Then laughs. HANNAH re-enters.

HANNAH: Will you take some wine, Rachel?

RACHEL: No, thank you.

HANNAH: Doesn't the Bible say something about taking a little wine for your stomach's sake? Sorrow?

SORROW: Yes . . . yes, please.

HANNAH: **(to RACHEL)** Just a little, eh?

RACHEL nods.

SORROW: Thank you.

HANNAH: Mister Chanterelle?

CLOON re-enters as HANNAH pours for GILBERT.

CLOON: Ah, the wine, splendid. **(HANNAH pours for him.)** Thank you, Hannah. Well, I propose a toast. To my dear wife. A man could never hope for so honest and capable companion. **(They toast her.)** Well, thank you all for coming, but I'm afraid that we have a train to catch.

GILBERT: Where to, Hannah?

HANNAH: It's to be a surprise.

CLOON: York tonight. Then Whitby.

HANNAH: Whitby?

GILBERT: Very nice. Have you been there before?

HANNAH: Yes.

CLOON: **(taken aback)** Have you, Hannah?

HANNAH: Yes, I was there, for a short time some years ago. Travelling.

CLOON: Oh. Well, I hope it has happy memories for you.

Anyway, Hannah, I shall go upstairs for the tickets. The cab should be waiting.

GILBERT: Is it a covered cab, John? It looks like rain.

CLOON: No, Gilbert. The sun is shining. I assure you.

RACHEL: We'll be off, Hannah.

CLOON: Goodbye, please do excuse me.

CLOON exits.

HANNAH: I'll see you out.

GILBERT: Like a good little servant. In the daytime.

HANNAH: **(taking SORROW's hand)** Come on.

They exit. GILBERT watches them go. He looks around the room. HANNAH returns, her face is red.

GILBERT: Have you been crying, Hannah?

HANNAH: No.

GILBERT: Was it hard to say goodbye . . . to your niece?

HANNAH: It's been an emotional day, sir.

GILBERT: **(quietly)** You're quite the little performer, aren't you.

She stares. CLOON re-enters with cases.

CLOON: Here we are.

HANNAH: Let me, John.

CLOON: Not at all.

GILBERT: John, we should talk . . .

CLOON: I'm sorry to hurry you, Gilbert, but we mustn't miss the train. Hannah, the cab is waiting.

GILBERT: Just one word. **(To HANNAH.)** Go and hold the cab, Hannah. I'm sorry, Mrs Cloon, Hannah, if you would.

HANNAH exits. CLOON speaks angrily.

CLOON: What on earth is it, Gilbert?

GILBERT: Nothing is what it seems. Be very careful.

CLOON: You cannot speak to me of care. And seeming.

GILBERT: **(pause, then)** No. Have a good trip. The best of luck to you both.

CLOON exits.

Scene 7

Doctor's study. GILBERT is being examined by DR MOFFAT.

DOCTOR: I'm afraid there can be no doubt, Mister Chanterelle. The symptoms of clumsiness, difficulty with arithmetic, and of course, the lesions on the skin around your lips . . . armpits . . . anus . . .

GILBERT: How long? I mean, how long have I been infected?

DOCTOR: It's impossible to say. It may be that you inherited it. Although, given your manner of life, other sources of uncleanness seem more likely. You're thinking of your wife, and children?

GILBERT: Yes.

DOCTOR: Well, as to your children . . . it may be several years. . . before any certain diagnosis can be effected. We can tell wives all kinds of things. The scabs can be attributed to

German measles . . . but the symptoms of general paralysis, the damage to the brain, to nerve and motor functions, I hardly think that a woman like Mrs. Chanterelle will remain in darkness for long.

GILBERT: What should I tell her?

DOCTOR: You're a dead man, Mister Chanterelle. I'm sure you know your own conscience better than I.

Scene 8

Whitby, the promenade. The sound and light of the seaside. Music is playing from a fair. A Juggler performs. CLOON and HANNAH, arm in arm, HANNAH still in her best dress, promenade.

CLOON: There seems to be a fair in town today. Would you not like to go along?

HANNAH: No, thank you, John.

CLOON: Perhaps you're right. Isn't the light wonderful?

HANNAH: Yes, John.

They pass the JUGGLER, who has been staring at HANNAH. She has been trying not to meet his eyes. As they pass, the JUGGLER starts.

JUGGLER: Hannah White, or God strike me dead. Hannah!

HANNAH: Hello, Arthur.

CLOON: Do you know this gentleman?

HANNAH: Yes, John.

JUGGLER: Know me, sir? Why wouldn't she know me? Ten years on the tramp together, sir, from Wick to Truro. . . . Why, Hannah White.

HANNAH: We were never on the tramp, Arthur.

JUGGLER: We were near it more than once. Winter of 48, d'you remember? Ourselves and the Irish fighting for potato scraps, and look at you now, Hannah, look at my Lady now.

HANNAH: This is my husband, Arthur. Mister Cloon of Edinburgh.

JUGGLER: Congratulations, sir . . . more than one of us tried to boat old Hannah White, but would she be landed? **(To HANNAH.)** D'you still do a turn, Hannah?

HANNAH: No, Arthur, not for a long time.

JUGGLER: Come now . . . **(He throws her three juggling balls.)** You never forget the mystery.

HANNAH: With your permission, John, of course.

CLOON: Yes . . .

HANNAH laughs apologetically, then juggles the three balls, glancing embarrassed at the astonished CLOON.

JUGGLER: **(to CLOON)** There we are, sir. It never leaves you quite.

CLOON: That was most impressive.

JUGGLER: That's nothing, sir. Bareback on a horse she used to do that, dressed in sky blue, skin tight, leading the troupe into town . . . she's been Lady Godiva and Cleopatra, in her time, sir . . . course, she was a little thinner then, weren't you, girl . . .

HANNAH: How are things, Arthur?

JUGGLER: You can see yourself how the motley fades, the teeth decay and the flesh slackens. But you've landed on your feet as neat as your dismount in the good old days.

HANNAH: Yes. John, will you give me your purse? **(CLOON hands her his money bag.)** Here, Arthur, be sure you share it.

JUGGLER: As always was, Hannah, a good and generous heart. **(To CLOON.)** You've a dazzler there sir, I hope you know it.

CLOON: I think I do.

JUGGLER: Are you in the trade yourself?

CLOON: No. I'm a civil servant.

JUGGLER: Funny, I could have sworn you was a poet. Good day to you.

He exits.

HANNAH: Did you think I'd been a servant all my life, John?

CLOON: You're so good at it. You seem to be good at many things

HANNAH: You turn yer hand to what you can.

CLOON: Do you still ride?

HANNAH: I took too many falls.

CLOON: I see. My new wife is a retired acrobat.

HANNAH: Yes. Shall we go down to the water?

CLOON: Hannah . . . why didn't you tell me before?

HANNAH: I didn't know that you'd be interested, John.

CLOON: I don't think that's true. I don't think you believe that. You concealed it from me.

HANNAH: Yes. John, I've done nothing in my life I'm ashamed

of . . . but I didn't know about you . . . whether you'd be ashamed. Are you ashamed of me?

CLOON: I'm astonished.

HANNAH: If you no longer feel obliged to me, John.

CLOON: It's not that . . . but you're a stranger to me. You frighten me.

HANNAH: Well, perhaps that's marriage after all. If I'd told you before, would it have changed your feelings?

CLOON: How can I answer that? You didn't tell me.

HANNAH: No, I didn't. I'm sorry.

CLOON: I'm sorry too.

HANNAH: John . . .

CLOON: No . . .

HANNAH: What are you thinking?

CLOON: Hannah . . . is there anything else you want to tell me.

HANNAH: You can be sure I love you, John.

CLOON: Yes. I'm sure I can. But we will take the train home tomorrow.

HANNAH: If that's what you want.

CLOON: I think I'll go for a little walk. I'll see you back at the hotel.

HANNAH: Yes, John.

CLOON leaves her.

HANNAH: Please God . . . Please God . . .

Scene 9

Chanterelle's house. Small parlour. GILBERT sits alone in the dark. ELIZABETH comes in, wearing street clothes. GILBERT wakes.

ELIZABETH: Did I wake you?

GILBERT: What time is it?

ELIZABETH: Just after three.

GILBERT: Morning or afternoon?

ELIZABETH: Afternoon. Shall I raise the blinds?

GILBERT: No, thank you.

ELIZABETH: Have you been here long?

GILBERT: I've been to see Doctor Moffat.

ELIZABETH: Have you?

GILBERT: I'm been thinking such strange thoughts. Doing such . . . unexpected things. But I think I understand them now.

ELIZABETH: What did he say?

GILBERT: Elizabeth, I think I've been ill for some time.

ELIZABETH: You've been working very hard. And staying out. . . . very late.

GILBERT: Do you still love me, Elizabeth?

ELIZABETH: Why are you asking me that? What's the matter?

GILBERT: It seems I have been suffering for some time from a degenerative illness from which there is no cure.

ELIZABETH: Don't be ridiculous.

GILBERT: He gave me this.

He holds a medicine bottle up for her. She takes it.

ELIZABETH: What is it? I can't read in this light. **(GILBERT gets up and lights a lamp. He brings it to her. She reads. Her face drains. She looks at him.)** No.

GILBERT: Yes

ELIZABETH: No . . . he's mistaken . . .

GILBERT: No. It explains a great deal of my behaviour.

ELIZABETH: No.

GILBERT: Doctor Moffat says . . . the disease is advanced. It may be . . . that even before we were married . . .

ELIZABETH: Our children . . .

GILBERT: Elizabeth . . .

ELIZABETH: Oh dear God . . . our children . . .

GILBERT: He can't say. We may both be gone, in any case, before we can know.

ELIZABETH looks at herself in horror. She begins scraping at herself with her hands. GILBERT watches as her fear and loathing overcome her. She recovers.

ELIZABETH: Syphilis?

GILBERT: Yes.

ELIZABETH: Have you killed me, Gilbert?

GILBERT: I should leave the house.

ELIZABETH: How dare you? How dare you frighten me like this?

GILBERT: You should burn my things.

ELIZABETH: **(takes the medicine bottle)** I'm going to pour this . . . away . . . and you'll stay at home . . . with me . . .

GILBERT: Elizabeth . . .

ELIZABETH: . . . how could you go to that fool Moffat?

GILBERT: I had good reason to believe in Doctor Moffat's discretion.

ELIZABETH: Is it to hurt me? You tell me this?

GILBERT: No, Elizabeth. I've never meant that.

He stands.

ELIZABETH: You're not going anywhere.

GILBERT: I couldn't bear you watching me die.

ELIZABETH: Don't spare me, please.

GILBERT: It's not you I'm thinking of.

ELIZABETH: Why are you punishing me? What did I do to you? Will you kiss me?

GILBERT: Would you really like that?

ELIZABETH: **(after a moment)** Yes.

They kiss passionately, as if embracing disease.

GILBERT: Shall I come to your bed now?

ELIZABETH: Yes.

GILBERT: No.

ELIZABETH: I'm already dead.

GILBERT: Yes. Say goodbye to the children for me.

ELIZABETH: **(attacking him)** You coward, you disgusting, filthy coward.

GILBERT: That's right. A little honesty. In the end.

He leaves. ELIZABETH sinks to the floor.

Scene 10

Waverley. At the station, CLOON has his bags taken by a porter and placed on a cart. HANNAH appears, dressed as a servant again. Her eyes meet CLOON's awkwardly. She looks down. CLOON looks away. CLOON exits. She and the porter follow with the bags.

Scene 11

Rachel's room. SORROW, holding a doll, wanders the room. She is bored. A baby is crying. SORROW walks over to one crib. She looks down. Then stares. Sniffs. She pokes a finger experimentally at the child. The crying stops. SORROW reaches in and lifts out the baby. She holds it at arms length. Then realizes that it's dead. She screams, dropping it. She screams again. RACHEL rushes in and sees her, sees the dead child. She goes over to it, picks it up. She looks at SORROW, and dandles the child as if it is alive. She places it back in its crib. She goes to console SORROW until she subsides.

Scene 12

Brothel. DAVEY and AGNES talk while a client, MISTER ALEXANDER, waits.

ALEXANDER: There'll be no screamin'. **(They look at him.)** I'll not have any screamin'

AGNES: **(to DAVEY)** Can I close my eyes?

ALEXANDER: I suppose so. But she's not tae move. Ye've told her that.

DAVEY: Mister Alexander. You've to promise Agnes now. She's not to be harmed.

ALEXANDER: I promise. **(To AGNES.)** So long as she understands. She's not to move. It spoils it if she moves. **(To DAVEY.)** Now can we get on?

DAVEY: Yes, yes. **(to AGNES)** Can't we, Agnes?

AGNES exits with Alexander. GILBERT enters.

DAVEY: Mister French?

GILBERT: Do you remember a girl called Agnes?

DAVEY: Agnes is busy at the moment, Mister French.

GILBERT: I only want to talk to her.

DAVEY: That's as maybe. Words also have their price.

GILBERT: It's words that damn us.

DAVEY: I don't disagree with you.

GILBERT: It is only the flesh that is truthful. That God made.

DAVEY: Right enough. 'He did not despise the Magdalene', Eh, Mister French?

GILBERT: I want to save her. If it's not too late. I want to save myself.

DAVEY: Perhaps you should have a glass of lemonade.

GILBERT: I'm talking about my soul. The burden on my soul.

DAVEY: Aye, well, there's a question of . . . her obligations.

GILBERT: What do you mean?

DAVEY: Well, we've been very accommodating with young Agnes. . . . we extended her credit. . . . There's the rent on that lovely room and there's the drink . . . and other things. . . . but she's workin hard to pay it all back. She doesnae want application, now that she's merr accustomed . . . to the hard facts of life. Nothing comes free in this world, Mister French.

GILBERT: I can settle what debts of hers remain.

DAVEY: Ye'll need to wait till Mister Alexander has had his turn.

GILBERT: Alexander . . . you're not serious. . . . the man's a lunatic . . . you gave him Agnes . . .

DAVEY: She was keen . . . he's a man who will meet the additional costs . . . of his unusual tastes . . .

GILBERT: **(ignoring him)** Agnes! Agnes! **(We hear AGNES screaming.)** Agnes!

DAVEY: Mister Alexander said no screaming! Agnes!

GILBERT: Agnes!

AGNES appears holding a knife She is covered with blood.

AGNES: Gilbert!

GILBERT: No.

AGNES: I didnae mean tae . . . **(GILBERT flees.)** Gilbert!

Scene 13

Cloon's House. CLOON sits in a chair, reading. HANNAH comes in, serving tea. She looks at him carefully, wondering. Their eyes don't meet. They are both desperately unhappy, and unsure how to repair the hurt. HANNAH goes to clean a sideboard. He looks at her. She meets his gaze now. The moment has come to speak. They still hesitate.

CLOON: **(eventually)** How did you do it?

HANNAH: What, John?

CLOON: Stand on a horse.

HANNAH: **(uncertain at first, then with growing confidence)** Well, ye have tae talk to a horse, whisper, nice and calm, like. Ye have tae tell it everything's gonnae be all right, ye see, then ye look in his eyes . . . and he says . . . **(Horse noise.)** . . . and that means he's listening, and then ye can tell him no one's gonnae hurt him, and ye hope he'll not hurt you, and ye hold him, by his mane, and ye keep holding, and ye keep talking until it seems natural, the maist natural thing in the world to jump up onto his back. **(She gets up on a seat, squatting, holding the mane.)** And ye say 'Now be you good to me, I'm letting go.' **(She stands, arms out, 'on the horse'.)** And ye stand, ye balance, ye feel his movement under ye, and yer feet just move wi him, and then yer up there, riding round and round, and everybody's lookin. Everybody's lookin at you. **(She steps down, demonstration over. She smiles shyly.)**

CLOON: I see. It must have been very exciting.

HANNAH: It was.

CLOON stands. She waits for him to come to her. He takes her hands, then they are together.

CLOON: Will you forgive me?

HANNAH: Yes. **(She considers a moment, then decides to speak. She has been thinking about this.)** You only ever have to ask me.

CLOON: What should I ask, Hannah?

HANNAH: I will keep nothing from you . . . John . . . if you ask me. If you want to know.

CLOON: You promise to keep nothing from me?

HANNAH: If you ask me. John. What is it . . . that I can tell you . . . that will keep you. You must be brave, John. You have to want the truth. Because you love me. If you love me, the truth can't hurt you, I promise you that. If you don't love me . . . then you don't deserve the truth. And I'll be your servant . . . not your wife.

CLOON: I don't know . . . what to ask you.

He is silent. She returns to her work.

Scene 14

Salisbury Crags. Some weeks later. ELIZABETH and LITTLEJOHN are walking. LITTLEJOHN is tired. ELIZABETH leads her father to a park bench. They sit.

ELIZABETH: Sit down, father. You are over exerting yourself.

LITTLEJOHN: It's a habit.

ELIZABETH: Are you still angry?

LITTLEJOHN: You're better off without him, damn his eyes, wherever he's hiding himself.

ELIZABETH: That's a little facile, isn't it, father? To dismiss twelve years of my marriage like that.

LITTLEJOHN: Now that you're free, Elizabeth. I feel I can tell you. Your husband enjoyed no good reputation among his peers.

ELIZABETH: Really, you feel you can tell me this now?

LITTLEJOHN: I am constrained to speak as a father should.

ELIZABETH: While before you were constrained to speak as a man, and say nothing at all.

LITTLEJOHN: A man and his wife . . .

ELIZABETH: A sacred bond, I know . . . a glade of paradise wooded around with secrets.

LITTLEJOHN: It was not my place.

ELIZABETH: Was I supposed to intuit his infidelities?

LITTLEJOHN: I didn't say that he was unfaithful to you.

ELIZABETH: But he was. You think?

LITTLEJOHN: Yes.

ELIZABETH: You're wrong. Gilbert was entirely faithful to his own nature. I knew his nature. I married it. He was always more uncomfortable about it than I was. He didn't understand himself.

LITTLEJOHN: And you did?

ELIZABETH: Yes, I think so.

LITTLEJOHN: And you persuaded me . . . over months . . . years, to let him marry you?

ELIZABETH: Yes. Gilbert means no harm to anyone but himself, father. That was always his way.

LITTLEJOH: Did you mean to save him?

ELIZABETH: Perhaps . . . but I think now, what I really enjoyed was watching him. A specimen of our age and your sex.

LITTLEJOHN: Are you so cold blooded?

ELIZABETH: I don't know. I've not had the leisure to wonder till now.

RACHEL, crazed, appears dragging SORROW behind her. She has a large bag over her shoulders.

RACHEL: Littlejohn! These are the last days.

ELIZABETH: Is this some friend of yours?

LITTLEJOHN: Who are you? How do you know me?

RACHEL: The world knows you, counter of things, thief of wisdom. Do not seek to know His creation lest His creation be taken from you. The last days, Littlejohn, mark it!

LITTLEJOHN: Oh, I see, Judgement Day is upon us, is it? We are all to go to hell?

RACHEL: You say it but do you know it?

LITTLEJOHN: How can you still exist?

ELIZABETH: Father . . .

LITTLEJOHN: No, I am sick of being shouted at by these savages. Madame, I promise you, for all of your delusions, you are a random agglomeration of chemicals randomly perpetuated on the basis of sexual selection. Which in your particular case, seems unlikely to continue.

RACHEL: Little man with swollen pride, your mind is the Red Whore that brings us to eternal death. The mountains will boil and the sky will fall before you know them as He knows them. I am not diminished by your taxonomy.

LITTLEJOHN: Look my dear, an educated lunatic.

RACHEL: You tell me I'm an accident. He tells me I am the created vessel of His love. Whom should I believe?

LITTLEJOHN: Believe who you like. Good day.

RACHEL: Are you so certain as you pretend? I can smell your fear, Littlejohn. You sweat, your doubt . . . but I stand certain in Jesus. You are crumbling before my majesty. Go! Your arguments mean nothing.

LITTLEJOHN: Not to a broken mind.

LITTLEJOHN and ELIZABETH exit. RACHEL takes the frightened SORROW, and sits her down.

RACHEL: There. The gentleman has given us his seat. Don't be frightened. Here. **(She opens her bag and produces two small rag dolls.)** We'll bury them here. This is a safe spot. Look at the view. When the avenging, fiery hand falls upon this Babylon, we will be safe here. Looking down . . . as we rise up from the flesh and its corruption. Help me dig.

They bury the dolls.

Scene 15

Tolbooth prison. The condemned cell. Some weeks later. Agnes is sitting on a cot in her condemned cell. The TURNKEY opens the door and we see CLOON and HANNAH struggling with the camera.

TURNKEY: I can give ye ten minutes.

CLOON: You can give us till we're finished.

AGNES: What's this? What do you want?

CLOON: Good morning. We've come to see you.

TURNKEY: They've come tae get a picture of yer neck, Agnes, for the anatomists tae look at. Before and after.

HANNAH: Hello, Agnes.

AGNES: Do I know you?

CLOON: I don't think so. I'm sorry for the intrusion.

TURNKEY: Ten minutes.

He exits.

AGNES: I'm sure I ken you fae somewhere.

CLOON: That's hardly likely.

HANNAH: How would you like her to sit, Mister Cloon?

AGNES: Cloon, that's it. Mister Cloon. I've seen you wi Mister Chanterelle.

CLOON: What? When? Where?

AGNES: At his hoose. I was . . .

She breaks down. CLOON signals to HANNAH.

HANNAH: What?

AGNES: I was his housemaid. It was nae merr'n two year ago.

She weeps.

CLOON: The Board of Governors have agreed that I should take your photograph.

AGNES: Why?

CLOON: I think, as an example to others . . .

AGNES: They want me on ma knees, dae they? Begging for

forgiveness? That man had a knife tae me and I took it tae him and by Christ I'd dae it again. No.

HANNAH: How would you like to be seen?

AGNES: What?

HANNAH: We don't want you on your knees.

AGNES: **(ignoring her, searching for, finding and showing a charcoal drawing of GILBERT)** Look. Have you seen him? Mister Chanterelle?

CLOON: No. He seems to be on holiday. He's been away for some weeks.

AGNES: I used tae think . . . a bit ae me used tae think he might come and see me. The stupid bit.

CLOON: I'm sorry. Could we . . . take the photograph now?

AGNES: Will ye get a message to him. **(Searching her cot.)** I've wrote him a letter.

CLOON: I haven't seen him, truly.

AGNES: Then fuck your photograph. You're lying, like the rest of them. **(She puts her face in her hands.)** All I did to him was love him.

HANNAH: *(sotto voce)* John?

CLOON: What?

HANNAH: Could we not take the letter?

CLOON: It's hardly our affair.

HANNAH: You disappoint me, John.

CLOON: I don't mean to.

HANNAH: To put the convenience of that gentleman above the wish of this dying girl.

CLOON: If you put it that way . . .

HANNAH: How else is there to put it? If you consider her feelings at all.

CLOON: **(to AGNES)** I'll try. But truthfully, he's not been seen.

HANNAH: Agnes. We could send a picture to your family.

CLOON: Hannah, really . . .

AGNES: Like this? Now?

HANNAH: Here.

HANNAH gives her apron to AGNES.

AGNES: I used to wear one just like this.

HANNAH: **(giving her bonnet)** Let me fix your hair.

AGNES: Thank you.

CLOON: Hannah, this is supposed to be an historical record.

HANNAH: It's how she wants her father and mother to see her. **(To AGNES.)** There. **(To CLOON.)** We're ready.

Music. CLOON takes an exposure counting ten seconds. AGNES' image as a servant appears on the screen.

CLOON: Thank you.

The TURNKEY rattles the cell door.

TURNKEY: That's yer time!

AGNES: One more . . .

CLOON: Now really . . .

AGNES: **(taking off her servant gear)** I want one more.

The TURNKEY rattles the door again.

TURNKEY: Time, now, please.

AGNES: Will ye send this one to Gilbert for me?

AGNES tries a naive, sexy, happy pose. CLOON hesitates.

HANNAH: **(tearfull)** Ach, Christ, John, will ye just take the lassie's picture?

Music. CLOON takes the exposure, counting ten seconds. AGNES' image appears on the screen, heroically maintaining prettiness. Music ends.

CLOON: There.

AGNES: Thank you, Mister Cloon. **(To HANNAH.)** Thank you. What's your name?

HANNAH: Hannah.

The women embrace as CLOON and the TURNKEY look on awkwardly. A bell begins to toll.

Scene 16

Execution. The previous scene breaks gently as the bell tolls. It is now the morning of the hanging. The cast gather as anonymous death watchers outside the prison gates. They are waiting for the bell to stop, which will be the signal that AGNES is dead. RACHEL and SORROW are among them . . . they are the only ones in character for the moment. It is raining, they are all covered with hoods.

RACHEL: **(to SORROW)** When the bells stops ringing, Sorrow, our poor sister is gone to Jesus.

The crowd wait. The bell stops. They wait for a moment, uncertain. Then a woman screams, pointing at one of the crowd who has fallen to the ground.

WOMAN: It's the plague! The plague!

RACHEL: A judgement. His judgement fall upon us now!

One of the crowd 'becomes' LITTLEJOHN. He examines the body.

LITTLEJOHN: **(to an OFFICIAL)** There's no doubt. It's cholera. Alert the militia. We must close the town.

The OFFICIAL and LITTLEJOHN exit. The rest of the crowd except RACHEL, SORROW and the GILBERT actor follow. RACHEL kneels by the corpse with SORROW.

RACHEL: Come Sorrow. Kiss her.

SORROW: No! I won't.

She flees. RACHEL follows, shouting.

RACHEL: Sorrow!

The GILBERT actor reveals his face, 'becoming' GILBERT, alone, frightened.

GILBERT: Agnes.

He exits.

Scene 17

Saint Giles. **A congregation of respectable people are gathered. They sing *God our help in Ages Past*. As they sing, GILBERT appears in the auditorium. He is weeping. The MINISTER rises to address the congregation, which includes the audience by extension.**

MINISTER: In this time of emergency, walking in the valley of the shadow of Death, men and women of good conscience may come into their strength. It is our unshakable faith that the Lord, using his instruments of science shall deliver us from evil.

GILBERT: **(distracted, from the congregation as if aloud to himself)** It's too late.

MINISTER: And we, my friends, can aid these officers of God's will. We must all remain calm.

GILBERT: She died.

MINISTER: We must keep order among ourselves, and impose order on those that will not keep it for themselves.

GILBERT: She died. It's too late.

MINISTER: It is distressing to us, no doubt, that sections of our ancient city have been closed to contain the infection . . . but such sanctions . . .

GILBERT: **(coming forward to the foot of the stage, now wanting to be heard)** They broke her.

MINISTER: This is a distressing time . . . I'm sure that our friend . . .

GILBERT: She was a child . . . she was God's child!

MINISTER: . . . will not want to disturb the children . . .

GILBERT: **(to the congregation/audience)** They broke her. They gave her to her Maker like a broken doll.

LITTLEJOHN: **(next to ELIZABETH, looks back, then)** It's him. It *is* him.

MINISTER: My friend, I must ask you to contain . . .

GILBERT: A broken doll . . . is that any way to treat God's child?

MINISTER: The gentleman must confine his grief. He must think of others.

GILBERT: I am thinking of others. I am thinking of all of you. All of you good people.

LITTLEJOHN: **(from his seat)** Sit down, you fool.

GILBERT: It's all my fault, you see. I dragged her into hell.

LITTLEJOHN: **(stands and turns)** Will you sit down and be quiet?

MINISTER: Dr Littlejohn, if you know this young man . . .

LITTLEJOHN: Know him? I've never seen him in my life.

He sits.

GILBERT: Elizabeth . . . I'm so sorry.

LITTLEJOHN: Elizabeth you will not talk to him.

ELIZABETH: **(stands)** Yes, Gilbert.

MINISTER: Dr Littlejohn, if the lady can calm . . .

GILBERT: Minister. Do you know where hell is?

MINISTER: Can he be removed, please.

GILBERT: I know where hell is. Hell is out there, locked down and confined. . . . Tell them the truth. Doctor Littlejohn, tell them where the cholera comes from . . .

MINISTER: This is not the time or place.

GILBERT: They are still drinking the water down there. They are still selling them water.

MINISTER: The community . . .

GILBERT: The community is dying from drinking its own shit. **(A man grabs him. GILBERT throws him off.)** I've seen you there. I've seen you in Hell. **(To a woman.)** Madame I have seen your husband down there in hell, rooting in his filth like a pig. **(To a girl.)** Pretty little girl, I have heard your father squeal. Like this 'weeee! weeee!'

LITTLEJOHN: He's mad.

GILBERT leaves the auditorium. The Minister tries to calm his flock.

MINISTER: Ladies and gentlemen. Please return to your seats. We must think mercifully of those deranged by grief.

LITTLEJOHN: Sit down, Elizabeth . . .

ELIZABETH: Goodbye, father.

LITTLEJOHN: Where are you going? Elizabeth!

ELIZABETH: Goodbye.

LITTLEJOHN: Elizabeth.

She leaves the auditorium in the same way GILBERT did.

Scene 18

Barricade. HANNAH is part of a crowd at a barrier guarded by militia. She tries to argue with a soldier.

HANNAH: My wee girl's in there . . . you've got to let me through. **(The soldier ignores her. She catches sight of LITTLEJOHN with papers in his hand, she fights her way towards him.)** Doctor Littlejohn, Doctor Littlejohn. **(She grabs him, he shakes her off.)** You know me, I'm Hannah White. I'm Mister Cloon's's servant. Hannah.

LITTLEJOHN: Hannah? What are you doing here?

HANNAH: My niece, Doctor Littlejohn, she lives in a house in College Wynd.

LITTLEJOHN: I'm afraid there's nothing to be done. The infection must be confined.

HANNAH: She's just a wee girl . . .

LITTLEJOHN: How old is she?

HANNAH: She's just nine.

LITTLEJOHN: In that case, she has an 80% chance of survival as opposed to 60% for a younger child.

HANNAH: Can I not go in and get her out?

LITTLEJOHN: I'm afraid not.

HANNAH: What if I said I would stay in there?

LITTLEJOHN: She has a eighty percent chance of survival, Hannah. Your presence would not improve that statistic. Excuse me.

He leaves her. HANNAH considers her next move.

Scene 19

The Chanterelles'. GILBERT sits holding a pistol. ELIZABETH comes to him. She sits beside him.

ELIZABETH: I've sent the children away with the servants.

GILBERT: Good.

ELIZABETH: I've written a note to my father. They'll find us together.

GILBERT: Yes.

ELIZABETH: It will be better this way.

GILBERT: No, I agree.

ELIZABETH pours liquid into two glasses.

ELIZABETH: It's a soporific. We'll feel nothing . . . but we'll be asleep.

GILBERT: I understand.

ELIZABETH: Will you tell me that you love me?

GILBERT: Elizabeth . . .

ELIZABETH: It doesn't have to be true.

GILBERT: All right. I love you.

They raise the cups to their mouths. She starts to drink. He doesn't. She hesitates. He looks at her and suddenly pushes her down to the sofa, a pillow over her face. He lies on top of her while she struggles. Then she is still.

GILBERT: I'm an honest man, Elizabeht. I'm the only honest man I know. If I lie, I can feel my tongue cleaving to my palette. I hear myself. Like an echo. I hear this thin voice. I see my pale, untrusting eyes looking at me in the mirror. Don't you know who I am? Can't you see who I am? I am full of ashes. Can't you hear it in my voice? Like some dead thing out of a cave? I hate lies. I hate the taste of them. It's dark in here now. It's full of bodies. The dark is full of bodies. Moving in the dark. Servile, silent skin. There is no sound. There are no faces. There is no my flesh, no your flesh. There is flesh and there is darkness. That's all. This is not my hand. This is not my face. This is not my voice. **(There is a sudden loud knocking.)** Already? **(The knocking continues as he stands and arranges himself for guests. He goes to the door and opens it. He sees HANNAH.)** Good evening. Am I expecting you?

HANNAH: I need your help, Mister Chanterelle.

GILBERT: You'd better come in.

HANNAH: I need to get into that house.

GILBERT: What house?

HANNAH: In College Wynd. The Old Town.

GILBERT: I don't know what you're talking about.

HANNAH: I've seen you there.

GILBERT: College Wynd?

HANNAH: Please don't pretend. The little girl . . . at the wedding . . . Sorrow.

GILBERT: Oh, yes?

HANNAH: They won't let me in. I've got to get her out of there.

GILBERT: I'm afraid it's not convenient. I'm expecting visitors.

HANNAH: You must know a way to get me in there. Just tell me.

GILBERT: I'm sorry, Hannah. I really don't think I can help you. Would you like a drink? Are you sure you won't come in?

HANNAH: What's wrong with you? It's her life. Perhaps I could speak to your wife.

GILBERT: She's not here. Go to your husband. He knows that place.

HANNAH: John?

GILBERT: He's been there. With me.

HANNAH: John? With you?

GILBERT: Why, yes. Of course he has. I'm very busy.

He closes the door. HANNAH goes into the street.

Scene 20

Street. HANNAH is accosted by a HAWKER with a cart.

HAWKER: So yer wantin intae the Auld Toon?

HANNAH: Yes.

HAWKER: There are ways.

HANNAH: Can you tell me?

HAWKER: It'll cost ye.

HANNAH: I don't have any money.

HAWKER: You can get it. Yer a servant . . . hint ye . . . in wan ae they big hooses?

HANNAH: Yes.

HAWKER: Then ye can get it.

HANNAH: I'm not a thief.

HAWKER: What's a thief nooadays, eh? Ye got somebody in there, have ye?

HANNAH: Yes.

HAWKER: Somebody ye want oot? Then ye can get it. Ye'll aye find me.

He moves on.

Scene 21

Cloon's house. CLOON is pacing anxiously. HANNAH comes in.

CLOON: Where have ye been? I've been frantic.

HANNAH: John. I must get into the Old Town

CLOON: Why?

HANNAH: You remember my niece. She'll die.

CLOON: Hannah . . . **(He embraces her.)** Don't you see it's not possible. We have to protect the public health.

HANNAH: What about her? What about all ae them in there?

CLOON: I know what you must be feeling. But it's not possible.

HANNAH: How dae ye know what I'm feeling? Ye don't know anything. She's my daughter. D'ye understand? That girl, Sorrow, she's not my niece, she's my daughter.

CLOON: She's . . .

HANNAH: She's mine. She's my flesh and blood.

CLOON: Your daughter?

HANNAH: I was going to tell you . . . when the time was right, but now I can't wait. I'm sorry. Help me.

CLOON: Are you already married? Do you a husband somewhere?

HANNAH: No . . . John, please . . . she'll die.

CLOON: No. Who are you? What are you? What kind of monster are you?

HANNAH: I lied to you. I'm sorry.

CLOON: You lied. It was all lies. I trusted you. I asked you to forgive me for doubting you.

HANNAH: I know.

CLOON: And you let me . . . when all the time . . . you can't stay here. You must leave.

HANNAH: I love you . . .

CLOON: How can I believe you? How can I believe my own feelings when you have so . . .

HANNAH: Please . . .

CLOON: . . . brazenly deceived me? I can't look at you. **(He takes one of his portraits of HANNAH and smashes it against a chair.)** Kindly don't say anything. You horrify me.

HANNAH: John . . . my husband . . .

CLOON: No!

HANNAH: **(clutching at him)** I beg you.

CLOON: Don't. Let go of me.

HANNAH: Master . . .

CLOON: Keep away from me.

HANNAH: You've been there. You've been in that house. Mister Chanterelle told me, you've been in that house . . .

He stares at her, horrified then exits. HANNAH recovers. She

opens a drawer and takes out handfuls of silverware. She exits. After a moment, CLOON emerges. He sees the open drawer. He stands looking into it, his mind racing. Then.

CLOON: Hannah!

Scene 22

The Breathing House. Women's voices sing a hymn. RACHEL crouches with SORROW.

RACHEL: Only with fire. Ye can see that, can't ye.

SORROW: Yer hurting me.

RACHEL: We are eaten with contagion here on earth.

SORROW: Please let go.

RACHEL: I blame myself. The signs were so clear. Sorrow.

SORROW: Why d'ye call me that? I hate that name. Everybody laughs at me.

RACHEL: This contagion . . . don't you see how clear it is? His Kingdom will come when the flesh is purged . . .

She lights a torch.

SORROW: You're scaring me.

RACHEL: Oh, no. . . . no. I don't mean to scare you. I don't mean to scare anyone. I'm doing this for you. I don't expect you to understand. But when He comes back, Sorrow, He will understand. And we'll see his face together.

She sets a fire.

SORROW: What are you doing?

RACHEL: Now you're not to worry. It's beautiful, Sorrow, look at it. See how pretty the fire is.

SORROW: Let me out. Let me out.

The fire rises. Singing continues.

Scene 23

Street. CLOON is rushing down the street. He meets GILBERT.

GILBERT: John, where are you rushing to.

CLOON: GILBERT, that house. I need to find that house. I've made a terrible mistake.

GILBERT: What house?

CLOON: Where you took me.

GILBERT: I never took you anywhere.

CLOON: You don't understand. Hannah has gone there to fetch her little girl. Her daughter, Gilbert.

GILBERT: I know.

CLOON: You know?

GILBERT: Yes. She came to me an hour or so ago.

CLOON: You knew?

GILBERT: About her daughter? Of course I did, it was obvious. Any fool could have seen it. You mean to say? . . .

CLOON: I am that fool. Yes. I am the greatest fool alive. Please, Gilbert, help me find her.

GILBERT: You love her, don't you?

CLOON: Yes. I do.

GILBERT: Then, of course I'll help you. Come this way.

Scene 24

The Breathing House. Singing continues, now joined by the sounds of fire, panic, tumult, and HANNAH, hammering on RACHEL's door. RACHEL sings.

HANNAH: **(off)** Rachel, please!

RACHEL: Sing with me, Sorrow.

SORROW: It's Auntie Hannah . . . let her in . . .

RACHEL: That's good.

The fire flares. SORROW grabs the keys from RACHEL, who snatches at her.

RACHEL: Sorrow, come back here.

The door breaks in. HANNAH enters with DAVEY.

DAVEY: Miss Rachel, get out of here.

RACHEL: **(holding SORROW)** Hannah.

HANNAH: Sorrow, come here . . .

RACHEL: Sorrow, this is Hannah. She is your mother. She is a whore. **(To HANNAH.)** There. That's all cleared up now.

HANNAH lunges at RACHEL. They struggle.

HANNAH: Take her, Davey . . . get her out!

DAVEY: Rachel . . . darlin . . .

Scene 25

Old Town. Street. GILBERT and CLOON are outside the burning building. A MILITIAMAN holds them back.

CLOON: Hannah! Hannah!

MILITIAMAN: Stay back, sir.

CLOON: My wife is in there! Hannah!

LITTLEJOHN approaches.

LITTLEJOHN: Officer! **(He indicates GILBERT.)** Hold that man!

CLOON: Doctor, make them let me in there. Hannah is in there.

LITTLEJOHN: Don't be ridiculous, man . . . they're all dead in there. **(To GILBERT.)** You, sir? You dare show your face?

CLOON: Sir, I'm sorry, but Hannah is in there. My wife, sir. My wife and child.

LITTLEJOHN: What? What are you people? Your wife?

GILBERT breaks free.

GILBERT: John, I'll save them . . .

He rushes into the house.

CLOON: Gilbert!

LITTLEJOHN: Burn, damn you. Burn in hell if you want to.

CLOON rushes toward the building, but is beaten back by the flames. He falls to his knees.

CLOON: Hannah!

The fire continues to burn. There is a great crashing as the building collapses in darkness. Then the light of the sun penetrates the gloom, illuminating CLOON and LITTLEJOHN.

Scene 26

Cloon's house, twelve years later. CLOON, now an old man, sits in his chair. A male servant brings in a letter. Hannah's picture, repaired, is on display.

SERVANT: This letter has come for you, Mister Cloon. Can I serve you with anything?

CLOON does not reply. He opens the letter. We hear HANNAH's voice. Perhaps see her at some other part of the stage, perhaps at work with washing.

HANNAH's VOICE: Dear John, I'm not sure how to address you, after twelve years, so the most human term will do.

CLOON stands unsteadily. He reads.

HANNAH's VOICE: I am truly sorry about deceiving you, and then deceiving you once more, but I thought it best that I should leave and not trouble you again. It is only now that I feel that we are safe, and I have nothing more to fear, that I can write these words.

CLOON rings for his SERVANT. He reads.

HANNAH's VOICE: I am an old woman now. You are an old man. I still have friends who are servants in town, and I have asked them to keep me informed about you. I am glad to hear that you are well.

The SERVANT enters.

CLOON: William . . . would you bring my coat please?

The SERVANT exits. CLOON reads.

HANNAH's VOICE: My little girl, who you knew as Sorrow, is married now. Her name is Grace.

We see SORROW, now 22, with a young man.

HANNAH'S VOICE: They have a son. He is very bonny.

The servant enters with CLOON's coat, and helps him on with it. CLOON reads.

HANNAH's VOICE: They work together as schoolteachers here in Cramond. I taught her myself, so you will be pleased to know your efforts with me did not fall upon stony ground.

CLOON: Cramond . . . **(To servant.)** Would you please hail me a cab?

He reads.

HANNAH's VOICE: They run a free school together for the children of Labourers. In the summer, their political friends bring slum children here. It would do your heart good to see them in the clean sunshine, singing.

CLOON exits.

Scene 27

HANNAH's house at Cramond. HANNAH, working at her washing, continues the letter we have heard.

HANNAH: I have not told them I am writing to you. They have very strict opinions about things. They scold me sometimes for doing too much for them. They say I am too much a servant, and that in the new world that is coming there will be no masters and servants anymore.

SORROW AS ADULT: **(from another room)** Mother!

HANNAH: Perhaps they are right. In any case, I did not want to go to my grave with their being any secrets between us. I am well and happy, and hope you are too. I will understand if I receive no reply. I remain your faithful Hannah.

SORROW AS ADULT: **(entering)** Mother.

HANNAH: Yes, Grace.

CLOON enters. HANNAH stands.

SORROW AS ADULT: This gentleman is here to see you. **(To CLOON.)** Whom may I say?

CLOON: I hope you may say . . . I am her husband.

HANNAH and CLOON look at each other.

The End

Losing Alec

Peter Arnott

'This fine, subtle play allows us to see those things not appreciated by the luckless characters, and perhaps to understand and forgive. The work uses a fantasy situation to dissect reality in a way realism never could, offering a dissection of the inadequacy of the emotional vocabulary in use in Scotland and voicing a protest against those responsible for that situation. And if it is set in Scotland, its resonances can be felt far beyond.'

Joseph Farrell, literary critic

'Calls to mind no less a dramatist than Arthur Miller.'

Allen Wright, The Scotsman

ISBN 978-0-9551246-3-1

£6.99

Web orders at **www.fairplaypress.co.uk**

Scottish **Arts** Council

Parking Lot in Pittsburgh

Anne Downie

'A piercing and funny look at how families control. Anne Downie's play rapidly transcends its own tight focus exposing us to wider issues and the abject hypocrisy of which we can all be guilty.

Moving, tender, tragic. Be prepared to laugh, weep and squirm!'

The Stage

'An appealing mixture of comedy and pathos that straddles continents as well as emotions. Intriguing that Anne Downie has taken individual notions of independence and co-dependence and used them as a metaphor for a country forever on the cusp. The extended routine on hormone replacement therapy is priceless!'

The Herald

'The strongest aspect of the writing lies in its treatment of the reality of emigration and the devastating accuracy of the relationships between the five sisters. Engaging human drama.'

The Guardian

ISBN 978-0-9551246-5-5

£6.99

Web orders at **www.fairplaypress.co.uk**

 Scottish **Arts** Council

The White Bird Passes

Anne Downie

adapted from the novel by Jessie Kesson

'The most eye catching aspect of Downie's play is its capacity, recalling O'Casey, to portray the life of a colourful community. The work, which eschews facile sentimentality, gives voice to a wealth of striking characters and is a gripping and moving one.'

The Scotsman

'The sheer energy and purity of Kesson's vision, captured in Anne Downie's stage version, is irresistible. The story comes as a reminder that no human being has to be defined by what society calls disadvantage. *The White Bird* not only passes but soars!'

Scotland on Sunday

'Anne Downie's effective, faithful and ultimately heart-rending adaptation of Jessie Kesson's novel, a classic of Scottish literature . . . changes the perception that Scottish Theatre is about urban, usually Glasgow working class life and evokes a world just as vibrant and ruthless, where hardship and tragedy lie unmawkishly beside beauty and undauntable humanity.'

The Guardian

ISBN 978-0-9551246-7-9

£6.99

Web orders at **www.fairplaypress.co.uk**

Scottish **Arts** Council

The Yellow on the Broom

Anne Downie

based on the novel by Betsy Whyte

'It can be no easy thing to find yourself, as travelling folk in Scotland long have, simultaneously the repository of conventional people's romanticism and the focus of their dark fears. It takes a real dramatist like Anne Downie, with her rich, enchanting and moving new play *The Yellow On The Broom* to give full expression to both aspects.

The lyrical lilt, the variety and vividness of character and scene make for memorable theatre.'

The Scotsman

'By turns heartwarming, painful, humorous and rousing. Above all it seems to grasp the essence of the travelling lifestyle. The play's ultimate form leaves one moved.'

The List

'A remarkable derivation by Anne Downie of Betsy Whyte's popular autobiography. The piece adroitly moves through time, using scenes, songs, and poetry to depict surprisingly interesting vignettes of everyday life on the road. A powerful memorial to the last days of the travelling people.'

Scotland on Sunday

ISBN 978-0-9551246-6-2

£6.99

Web orders at **www.fairplaypress.co.uk**

Scottish **Arts** Council

27978127R00072

Printed in Great Britain
by Amazon